What Heaven Is Like

By

Jane Lea Dykstra

ISBN-978-0-615-61375-8

DEDICATION

I dedicate this book to my beloved Mom and Dad,
Mel Dykstra and *Jeneane Dykstra*.
You are amazing parents
and the answer to every child's dream.
I love you very much.
Forever, Jane

In addition, I dedicate this book to you,
Richard Powers Moe
You are my soul mate for eternity.
I love you, Jane

TABLE OF CONTENTS

ACKNOWLEDGEMENTS

I would like to thank my beloved Dad and Mom, **Mel and Jeneane Dykstra**, for teaching me about Faith. You will always be the Angels on my shoulders.

I would like to say thank you, **Richard Powers Moe**, for always being there for me. You have never let me down and you have become the best part of my life.

Thank you so much, **Daniel R. Dykstra,** for all your tireless hours teaching me how to work within the proper structures of a book and for all the things you have taught me about myself. You mean more to me than I can ever tell you and I cannot imagine life without you. I thank God every day for the knowledge that I will never have to be without you.

I would like to say thank you, **Grace Dykstra**, for being such a great friend and for your wonderful, never-ending spiritual advice.

Thank you, **Becky Jo Dykstra**; you are a gift from God. You are one of the few people in the world a friend can always count on to be there when we call out your name

Thank you, **Chanelle Innis**, for the gift of you. My heart will never let go.

Thank you, **Kristina Dykstra, Desiree Dykstra, Dana Dykstra, Terry Dykstra, Peggy Dykstra, and Jack Huang,** for everything you are to me.

I would especially like to thank **Kilmer Oscar Moe Sr., Mable Lane Moe, Lillian 'Special' Moe, Kilmer Oscar Moe Jr., Marjorie Jane Powers Moe, Mildred Rupert Powers, and Robert Irvin Powers**, because without your beautiful visions this book would not exist.

I would like to thank you, **Steve Pendleton, Pendleton Construction**, for all your patience while Richard is here with me, and the kindness you share with everyone you meet.

Thank you very much to **Robert Kilmer Mo**e, **Robin Culver**, and *Kathy Lane Moe,* for your wonderful pictures.

Last, but never least, I want to say thank you to my beloved cat, *Faith*. I could not have done anything without you.

I love you all, Jane

INTRODUCTION

Do you have a loved one who has passed on? Do you wish you could talk to them again? Would you like to tell someone you have lost how very much you love them?

You can. When a loved one becomes an Angel, they come back to you. Your loved ones can hear you and they can see you. You can learn to talk to your Angels and hear them as well. This ability to communicate with your dearly departed is a gift that God has given to all his beloved children. You can use your gift not just once, not just in your dreams, but today and every day as often as you wish.

This book is a journey into my life with the Angels on my shoulders. After an accident, I learned to chat with these amazing spirits that have passed on. My gift of communicating with the dearly departed is not from a near-death experience. Nor has it been a one-time occurrence. I am still in contact with these beautiful Angels in a way that has changed my life. I believe that by reading this book it can change your life as well.

You know that feeling that comes over you sometimes when you sense that you are not alone, however, you look around, and no one is there. Have you ever had an experience when you knew 'I should or I shouldn't' do this or that. If you look back to those occasions, you will remember that you heard a 'little voice' inside giving you a warning. That 'little voice' is one of your own special Angels whispering in your ear trying to guide you carefully through life. Now I know that this 'little voice' or 'sixth sense' is a gift, a form of communication between those that have passed on, and you. We all have this wonderful gift and you can develop it to fit your own needs. You can learn to communicate with your dearly departed just as I have. The way you listen, the way you talk to your own Angels, is as individual as you are.

Through this incredible journey I am about to take you on, you will learn what I have learned; that your beloveds are still a part of your life. They are with you and they are waiting for you to sense them so that you will talk to them. Your loved ones certainly want to talk to you. Best of all I have learned this gift of communicating with the Angels is not difficult. Your loved ones are right there on your shoulders. They want you to know they have never let go of you and they never will.

This book is a true story written from my heart. I did not intend to write a book, these memories are a gift I shared only with those close to me. When my visions first started, I felt confused and uncertain. I did not understand. These doubts remained with me for eighteen months after the visions began. I tried to explain to outsiders what I was seeing but they dismiss my visions as unlikely illusions. For answers, I turned to God and He set me free from the opinions of others. I saw the truth and I began to enjoy my gift.

Now five years later, I have felt a calling from God to share my lessons with others. God wants all his cherished children to develop the gift He has given them, the gift of communication with your own special Angels.

I have written this book so that you will get to know the Angels who appear to me as I have. The memories in these chapters are all from my visits with the dearly departed. I will share with you stories from my visions followed by transcripts of taped recordings. These tapes are the actual visions as they took place and as recorded by my fiancé, Richard Powers Moe.

My visions began with people I have never met. When these Angels came to me, I soon realized they were the dearly departed of my fiancé, Richard, who began recording my visions nearly five years ago. Richard continues to record to this day because he does not want to miss one wonderful word from his loved ones.

If you would like to hear the live recordings utilized in this book, I would like to invite you to visit http://www.whatheavenislike.com. On our website, you will find other visions as well as additional photos, stories, and testimonials.

I have felt a need to believe in myself so to the best of my ability; I have verified the information in the recordings.

I will have met my goal in writing this book when God answers my prayers. I pray that you find the same peace in your mind and in your soul that I have found.

I pray you may find joy in knowing your loved ones are still with you and that your paths will forever be as one.

Please, take my hand. I am so excited to share this gift with you.

ABOUT RECORDED VISIONS

Included in the Table of Contents is a list of transcripts from my taped recordings. These recordings are from my visions and I have included these transcripts so that you will get to know these beautiful spirits as both people, and as the Angels they have become. The visions I have included in the book became the background of the main characters in my chapters. They are all dearly departed family members of my fiancé, Richard Powers Moe.

Richard's Mother is Marjorie Jane Powers Moe, and I will refer to her as either 'the Mom' or 'Mom.' Richard's Dad is Kilmer Oscar Moe Jr., (a.k.a. Junior or Kim) and I refer to him as 'Dad.' Richard's paternal Grandfather is Kilmer Oscar Moe Sr., and I refer to him as 'Grandpa.' Richard's maternal Grandfather is Robert I. Powers, and I refer to him as 'the Robert.' Richard's maternal Grandmother is Mildred Rupert Powers, and I refer to her as 'the Mildred.' Mable Lane Moe is Richard's paternal Grandmother and I refer to her as 'the ornery Grandma' or 'Grandma.' Richard has an Aunt Lillian Moe, whom I refer to as 'the Lillian,' and Richard's beloved dog I refer to as 'Barney' or 'the Barn' Barney Powers Moe.

Please enjoy these recordings and find within yourself the Faith to believe as I have. Open the door so that your own dearly departed may walk into your dreams as well. Listen to the Angels on your shoulders; they are trying to talk to you. Above all may our beloved God bless you and all those you love.

Jane Lea Dykstra

PART I ANGELS ON MY SHOULDERS

CHAPTER 1 NEVER LET GO

"Richard, I saw your dad," I said through the fog the anesthesia created.

Richard kneels gently next to my gurney and tenderly takes my hand. Stroking my fingers Richard shakes his head to clear it believing he must have heard me wrong. A muscle tightens in Richard's stomach as he whispers, "Honey, what did you say?"

Richard leans in closer and whispers gently in my ear, "Sweetheart; my dad is dead remember?"

I continue to deliver words that would shake Richard's very soul, "Your dad told me to tell you that he had been in my dreams while they were operating on me. To convince you that I have seen him he said that his real name is Kilmer Oscar Moe Jr., although everyone called him 'Junior' or 'Kim.' Your dad told me that he was born in the Philippines and to remind you how much he hated to wear shoes."

Richard's mouth goes dry and his hands begin to tremble. He shakes his head in amazement because Richard knows he has never spoken to me about his father. The one exception was to tell me that his dad had died when he was only fifteen years old. Richard has shared with me that his dad had gone to the hospital for what should have been a routine procedure and never came home. Richard is stunned because what I just told him about his dad only he and his immediate family knew.

I continue my ramblings by turning to the nurse who is adjusting my IV bottle and I point to her. With excitement I exclaim, "You have Angels on your shoulders, a blue one, and a pink one!"

Richard turns to the nurse who is now wheeling me out of recovery. Out of the Richard's mouth popped the very words he is thinking, "Jane really did see my dad!"

The nurse smiles at Richard and responds by gently explaining, "We hear things like this all the time after a patient comes out of surgery."

Richard is sure they hear some strange things all right, but this. I am talking about a man I have never met. Richard believes I had visions of Angels during my surgery and he is hungry for more.

Richard turns to me with so many unanswered questions but remains quiet as I continue with my vision, "Richard, when I first saw your dad he was standing in the light smiling at me and he introduced himself by saying, 'Hello, Jane, I heard you talking to me last night. I am Richard's Dad.'"

Richard looks up at the nurse with these questions in his eyes. She smiles back at him knowingly and shrugs her shoulders.

Richard tenderly strokes my cheek as I continue, "Richard, your dad is so wonderful. He said to me,

'Please, Jane, do not be afraid. You are going to survive this surgery because it is not your time.'"

Closing my eyes I recall for Richard the rest of this beautiful vision, "As your dad stepped out of the light he continued his conversation by asking me, 'May I share something wonderful with you? I want you to feel how much God loves you.'"

"Richard, I felt as though your dad already knows me. He reached behind his back and said, 'I will barely open this door that contains His light, no more than that because you are not capable of understanding everything Heaven has to offer.'"

"Your dad opened this door a quarter of an inch and a light poured through. Within this light, I could feel God's love. I felt cherished and the intensity of that feeling was overwhelming. I will never forget that moment and I will no longer be afraid of dying."

Richard is quiet as he pulls the covers up and tucks them carefully around my shoulders. He is waiting for me to continue my story. "Richard, I reached toward that light and I stammered to your dad, 'It is so beautiful. I want to come with you!'"

"Your dad gently shook his head and explained, 'No, I am sorry but you must stay there for now. Please, Jane, take care of my son for me.' With a radiant smile he looked at me and I felt as though we began a special journey into the spiritual world."

Retelling my vision is exhausting and Richard can see I am starting to fall asleep. He kisses my forehead as I close my eyes and he tells me, "I love you, Honey. I will be here when you wake up."

The pain medication takes over and I start to drift off. I manage to mumble one final thought to Richard,

"The last thing I remember your dad saying to me was, 'Please, Jane, tell Richard to do as I have done; tell Richard to never let go!'"

CHAPTER 2 A STORY TO SHARE

Richard and I have been through one heck of a week. Several days earlier, I slipped on a wet manhole cover in the Hollywood Hills. I broke every bone in my left ankle. My ankle had come out of its socket and was dangling off to the side. The ambulance came and they took me to St. Joseph's Hospital where all the Emergency Room Physicians could do was set the bones back together. The doctors gave me a cast and then informed me that I will need surgery because my whole ankle had shattered. These wonderful physicians share with me that I will need a surgeon to sew all the bones in my ankle back together and they give me the names of several Orthopedic Surgeons whom they highly recommend.

I make an appointment to see the specialists on their list, one after another. These Surgeons take one look at my X-rays, shake their heads, and send me away telling me they could not repair the damage. I feel devastated and very depressed, not to mention the amount of pain my ankle is causing.

I would not have made it through this ordeal if not for my fiancé, Richard Powers Moe. Richard is a very kind, sensitive, and loving man. I want to give up on finding a doctor to help me but Richard will not hear of it.

With his usual patience and enthusiasm over me Richard announces, "Honey, I found another specialist for you to see."

With my usual lack of patience I retort, "No, I am not going!" I can be a little stubborn and Richard could see I have set my jaw. I did not want to go because each trip was absolute agony. After so many rejections, I felt hopeless.

Richard is my rock and he knows how to get around my jaw, "Honey, let's just get in the car and go there," he pleads. "If you don't want to get out of the car when we get there you don't have to."

Well, that sounds reasonable so I agree to take that step--anything to make him happy. Besides, I figure I can get out of it once I get there.

After a painful ride with Richard driving the car and me curled up in the backseat, we arrive at our destination. Richard holds out his hand and smiles, "Well, we're here. Let's go in."

Richard leaps out of the car and grabs my latest gift, the dreadful wheelchair. I hate that thing and I frown at him. Richard is just so excited over the prospect of healing me. He continues breathlessly as he heaves the heavy chair out of the car, "Then, if you don't like him we will go home."

I reluctantly accept his hand. Richard gently lifts me up and delivers me into my new form of transportation. The wheelchair has become my set of legs and I grumble all the way into the Doctor's office.

In agony, I wait to hear my name called. I try to ease the pain by lying on one of the doctor's thoughtfully provided sofas. I am expecting another refusal to fix me, and another grouchy person who shakes their head when they examine me. Finally, it is my turn and I hear my name called. To my amazement, my doctor was young and quite good looking. Wonder of wonders I did like him! Dr. Burns is one of the very fine Orthopedic Physicians from Southern California Orthopedic Institute in Valencia, California. This gentle man looks at my X-rays, turns to me with a twinkle in his eyes, and I began to see a glimmer of hope.

Doctor Burns begins by telling me ever so gently, "I believe I can put you back together again."

"Wow!" I respond excitedly, "I had given up."

Those eyes of his crinkle as he smiles at me and says, "Yes, but I want you to know it will be a very long surgery. It could take a long time for you to recover. However, with a lot of hard work on your part, I believe you can walk again."

I take a deep breath and begin to weep. Through tears, I look up at him and ask, "Why did this happen to me?"

Dr. Burns delivers the final blow, "I can also tell you that if you break your ankle again I may not be able to put it back together."

I feel very angry, depressed, and so sad. Richard drives me home from the doctor as I cry in the backseat and ask God, "Why, Father, why did this happen to me?" As I lay there feeling sorry for myself, I had no idea that my wonderful and amazing God has plans in store for me. As always in His Infinite wisdom, God has a message for me. It would take many years for me to see that God has a story that he wants me to share.

Dr. Burns schedules my surgery for two days later. I am terrified. Richard tucks me into our bed and tries to reassure me about the operation, "Honey, Dr. Burns does this kind of operation every day, and after that you can finally begin to heal."

I am in so much agony that I remain unconvinced. I retort, "Richard, your own father went into the hospital for what should have been just a routine procedure, and after vomiting into his own lungs your dad died there."

I was immediately sorry after I said this to him because Richard never talked about his parents. Both of their deaths were painful to him, especially his fathers. It was an unnecessary and unexpected tragedy, and so unfair to a fifteen year old.

I try to ease the pain I have caused Richard, "I am so sorry I said that to you, Honey."

I began to weep and said, "That is my biggest fear, Richard. My fear is that I might leave you, too!"

Wiping my eyes I add, "I am afraid the same thing will happen to me."

Richard turns his head but I see the tears that are spilling out of his own eyes. Later that evening I recall this conversation and I begin talking to Richard's Dad in my prayers. I tell him how sorry I am that he died so young, that I wish I could have known him, and please, to pray for me that I would be okay.

The morning of the surgery is a blur to me. I do not remember much about the preparation for the procedure that was to come other than pain and fear. Nor do I remember what I said to Richard about his dad or about seeing the Angels. What I do vividly remember is the actual vision itself. This vision is when I met Richard's Dad, saw the light for the first time, and began a new insight into life after death.

As Richard is driving me home from the day's ordeal, I keep thinking that I wanted to see this wonderful light again and chat some more with this dear man. How can I make it happen?

Richard delivers me into our bed with his usual care and attention. He fusses over me because he could see the pain written on my face. I am a mess. I cannot move from this huge cast on my leg, not even to go to the restroom.

Richard takes over as my legs. My wonderful man takes complete care of me. We have a construction company together and now Richard has to not only do his work, but mine as well--and he has to take complete care of me. I could do nothing to ease all the additional pressures that my accident has placed on Richard. My man never complains; he goes to work and comes home every night with a smile on his face. As a result, I feel so guilty during the time I am recovering from my injury.

Healing from major surgery requires many hours of sleep. It shields you from the pain and gives your body time to recover. I needed to heal from not only from my break, but from the reconstruction of my ankle as well. During my four-hour surgery, Doctor Burns had to imbed a six-inch long plate inside my ankle with eight screws to hold it in place. He also had to insert a six-inch screw through my heel and into my leg to keep my ankle together.   I received medications that sedates me and controls the pain. It would take a whole year for me to recover. I was bedridden for two months, in a wheel chair for six months, and needed a walker for another two months. Crutches came next followed by physical therapy. Finally, a year later I took my first unassisted steps.

All I can do to help Richard, and show him how much I care about him and all he is doing for us, is to get well as fast as I can. To accomplish this; I sleep a lot.

To my wonder the very first time I close my weary eyes Richard's Angels begin to take care of me. I am sleeping yet I hear a voice from somewhere say, "Hi, Jane, I am Richard's Grandfather, Kilmer Oscar Moe Sr."

I take it in stride because I am dreaming. Wait, there it is again. I hear a voice but this time the voice has a face, "You remember my son, of course. Here is Richard's Dad."

Peering at me intently was the face of a very handsome and gentle man. Kilmer Sr. has his arm around his son, Kilmer Oscar Moe Jr., and they both look at me to see if I recognize Kilmer Jr. from my surgery visions. Of course I do.

Smiling at them both, I murmur with excitement, "Yes, I remember you from the light. I wanted to go with you."

Kilmer Jr. is beaming and I can see he is pleased because I have not forgotten him. Kilmer Jr. reaches into the light and takes the hand of a woman. Drawing her forward, I can see she is beautiful and has an aura of pink.

"I would like you to meet someone very special. This is Richard's dear Mother, Marjorie Jane Powers Moe," said Kilmer Jr. "She wants to say, 'Hi,' to you, too. You both have so much in common besides our Richard."

As she steps out of the light, Marjorie Jane Powers Moe cups my face, kisses me on both cheeks, and says, "Dear, sweet Jane, I have waited so long for this moment. We are so excited you are here with us."

Marjorie Jane Moe slips an arm around my waist and continues, "We have been trying to reach you and our dear son, Richard, for so long. I want to thank you for giving us this wonderful opportunity."

Tears begin to slip down Marjorie's cheeks as she adds softly, "Your faith gave us the steps to reach you when you began to pray to Jesus the night before your surgery. Jesus heard your prayers, and your fears, and sent Richard's Dad to comfort you." I look at Marjorie feeling giddy inside. I already felt so loved by Richard's dearly departed family.

Grandpa Moe slips his arm around my shoulders and shares his thoughts; "You were so open to my son, Kilmer Oscar Moe Jr., that he was able to slip into your dreams during surgery."

Wow, this is quite a dream. I never want to wake up. To make it even better Kilmer Jr. cradles my face between his hands and says to me, "Now that you are here we want you to know you can come back as often as you wish."

Kilmer Jr. kisses my forehead and shares even more, "We will be here waiting with open arms and open hearts. Do not worry about how you will come back to us. Once you make it here, your subconscious mind remembers the way back. Please visit soon because the rest of our family is so excited for you to meet them."

I look at him as I shake my head. "Come back here, are you kidding." I whisper my thoughts to him in awe, "I never want to leave!"

Richard's Mom still has her arm around my waist. She makes me feel like a treasured child and finishes the thought that her husband has started, "The rest of Richard's family have already seen you of course, but now you will be able to see them. You have opened your hearts to us and now we can share with you, and with our beloved Richard, how wonderful it is to have the gift of Heaven. We want to take you to our home, which we have recreated in the likeness of Hawaii. Everything we loved when we lived in our bodies is here with us. We have the ability to share with you some of the wonders that awaits you when you arrive in Heaven. We will have fun and show you our favorite places like Ice Cream Alley and Candy Cane Lane."

Marjorie Jane Powers Moe continues, "Our beloved pets are with us as well. Richard's German Shepherd, Barney, can sense you, and wants to be with you. We have always been a part of your life ever since you became part of our son's life, and we have never let go."

With a warm smile Marjorie continues, "When you lose a loved one from within their bodies their spirit can still spend time with you. The spirit of your loved one is the same person you knew before their bodies died. God knows the sorrow we feel when a loved one dies so He gave us all the gift of continued interaction with our dearly departed. Some of God's children are aware of their gift and spend time with their loved ones who has passed on. They can talk to their Angels and when they listen, they can hear their Angels as well."

"To develop this gift you must recognize and believe we are still with you. We have a message from Jesus to share with everyone who has lost someone they love; believe in yourself. If you have sensed the presence of your dearly departed before, accept that what you are feeling is real. Once you become aware of the Angels on your shoulders we will come to you any time you call our names."

"You are not unique in having this gift, Jane, just blessed to see your gift so clearly. Kilmer Jr., Kilmer Sr., and I are trained teachers. Jesus has asked that we teach you how to use your gift. First, you must accept our truth and believe in yourself. When the time is right you will share this story and you will know your day to spread His word has arrived."

I look at this incredible woman with tears in my eyes and I respond, "Those are the most beautiful words anyone has ever said to me." It is a very emotional moment.

I begin to cry and Richard's Grandfather, Kilmer Sr., lightens the mood by twirling around and around and saying, "See? We don't have wings!"

I have to laugh at that one and as I wipe my tears, I tell him, "Yes, I always thought Angels had wings."

Kilmer Jr. chuckles and assures me, "We could have wings if we want to."

Marjorie, always the loving mother, touches my forehead and says with a worry, "We have kept you here long enough. You need your rest now, dear one, so we are going to send you back to your other dreams for some deep sleep."

Marjorie's face lights up when she smiles and she says with a tease, "Please tell Richard that I want to know when you two are going to give me a Grandchild?"

Richard's Grandfather Moe winks at Marjory and adds with his own chuckle, "Yes, please tell him I would love a Great-Grandchild, too." Kilmer Sr. reminds me of Santa Claus. He is so jolly and his laugh comes from his belly. I feel so at peace with my new friends. I do not want to leave. I do not want to wake up. Of course, I have to. Someone is shaking my shoulders.

CHAPTER 3 HEAVEN IS WONDERFUL

Richard peers at me and pulls me from under the covers, "Honey, how are you feeling?"

"Richard, I was just dreaming that I met your Grandpa Moe," I answer sleepily. "Oh, and Richard, I met your Mom."

I drag myself up onto the pillow and continue, "I love her. I feel so close to her already. Your mom has so much energy, Richard. I love the way she loves you. When your mom wakes up in the morning, she stretches just like a cat. I love the way your mom sneezes, 'Achoo, Achoo, Achoo, Achoo, Achoo, Achoo.' She eats corn-on-the-cob like a typewriter."

Richard's mouth begins to hang open but I do not even notice it. I rush on with my vision, "Your mom is so beautiful, and she smells so good. I asked your mom what kind of perfume she wears and your mom answered, 'It's Richards's's favorite, 'White Shoulders.'"

Now Richard's mouth has dropped to his chin and he rubs his face. Richard does not get a word in edgewise, though. I continue to stun him by saying,

"Your mom is so in love with your dad and your dad; he adores your mom. He looks at her like she is a lollipop."

Then I add, "Dad calls your mom his soul mate." I am breathless with excitement. I cannot tell Richard my story fast enough.

Richard sits down on the bed and put his hand on my forehead, "Are you feeling okay, Honey? Do you need a pain pill?" Richard looks at me, worried, as he always is where I am concerned.

I shake my head, "No. I had a pill about two hours ago." I roll my eyes at him, "Did you hear what I said? I met your mom. She showed me her greenhouses with all the Orchids and she fussed over me like I was one of her own."

Richard is looking pained so I go on to reassure him, "It's okay, Honey, when I pointed this out to your mom she pulled me close and said, 'Well, you are one of my own and you always will be.'"

I continue to explain to Richard as if he does not know his own mom, "She is like a little girl. Your mom is so excited about absolutely everything."

Richard's eyes begin to fill with tears. He whispers to me, "Jane, what can this mean? How can this be real? You have never met Mom yet you are describing her as if she were standing here." Now with real sobs, my wonderful man takes me in his arms.

I hug him back and look into his eyes. I ask him, "Do you believe me, Richard? Do you believe in my dreams?"

Richard takes my hand in his and whispers into my ear, "I believe you, Honey. I believe you with every ounce of my soul."

Richard leans up on one elbow and adds with worry, "I just hope they will come back."

My Angels do come back. They come to visit me the next night, the next, and every night since. Richard works hard all day, taking the burden of both our work onto his dependable shoulders. At the end of the workday, however, Richard races home to be by my side. Bounding up the stairs and landing in our bed, Richard shares his day. During his recital, I can feel myself drifting away but I try to stay focused.

Peering at me intently Richard asks, "How was your day, Honey?"

I look at him as if he has lost his mind. I am stuck in bed with a huge cast, cannot even move, and I am in constant pain.

I respond with a teary, "Richard, my life is filled with agony, sleep, and medications."

With a sigh I continue, "The only things I have to look forward to all day long are you and my visions. Praise the Lord!"

Richard nods his head in agreement, "Honey, I know sleeping gives you a break from the constant pain."

Knowing when to change the subject, Richard does so. "Honey, what did you dream about today?"

Now Richard has my full attention. I pull myself up to a sitting position and breathless from the exertion; I share my new visions.

"Richard, today I met your Uncle Harold," I said with excitement.

Richard fluffs the pillows behind my head and asks, "Dad's oldest brother was with you?"

Grateful for his attention I answer, "Yes, he is so sweet. I love everyone there." Richard begins to rub my shoulders as I continue, "Harold told me a story because he wants you to know it is really him. Harold told me about the time that he taught you and your sister, Kathryn, to play Marco's Polo in your swimming pool on Vose Street. Harold said to ask you if Kathryn would put her head under the water yet."

With a chuckle Richard answers me, "No, to this day I don't believe my sister will duck her head all the way in."

I continue with my memories, "I also met Harold's son, Paul. Harold and Paul died together in a fire. Paul just got there."

Richard is looking at me strangely so I stop with my story and ask him, "Are you okay, Honey?"

Richard takes my hand and answers, "I'm all right. Please, go on."

I am surprised at the look in his eyes and it's with hesitation that I continue, "I don't know where Paul has been, but he didn't get the gift until just recently. I think it has something to do with the way Paul and Harold died."

Richard is quiet and waiting for more so I continue, "Your mom, dad, Lillian, and I went for a race in the Magic Teacups and then we got to go to Ice Cream Alley. It was so much fun!"

Now Richard is smiling again and I explain to him, "Ice Cream Alley is where you swim in the ice cream. You just take a lick from every kind of ice cream there is and then when you want a topping, you scoop it up and dump it on the next lick."

Feeling the excitement from my dreams, I sit up and continue, "There are candy toppings and nut toppings in Ice Cream Alley, the best of everything!"

Richards's eyes crinkle as he smiles at me, "Wow," he says, "Heaven sounds like a wonderful place." Then he adds, "What are Magic Teacups?"

Closing my eyes as I remember the best dream, I tell him, "In Heaven everyone spends their time with family and friends. They get together and do all sorts of fun things. One of the fun things they do is racing each other in these teacups that have wings."

Richard is amused and lets me go on, "We fly around the stars and the sun. When we pass the moon, we reach out and grab a bite of cheese. Whoever wins the race gets to wear a blue ribbon and ride in the front of the next parade."

Finding myself exhausted, I decide to lie back on my pillows. Sensing something is bothering Richard I ask him, "Why were you looking at me like that when I told you about your cousin, Paul?"

Richard puts my hand back on the sheets and begins pacing the room. Finally, he turns to me and asks, "What did you mean when you said Paul had just got there? Harold and Paul both died in a fire at their home at the same time."

Reflecting back to my dream I try to remember if I know the answer. Finally, I said, "I only know that Paul had died with Harold but while Harold came right to the gift, Paul had to wait."

Hoping Richard has some insight I look at him. Richard sits back on the bed beside me and wonders aloud as he says, "Maybe it has something to do with the fact that Paul may have caused the fire. They think

37

Paul was smoking in bed but they know it was an accident."

I look to Richard for clarification but he is shrugging his shoulders. I return his shrug and say, "Do you think Paul could have been in Purgatory or something?"

We do not have the answer and fall into silence, each with their thoughts. Finally, I have a question for Richard, "So it's true, they did die in a fire?"

Before he can answer I also ask, "Is it true, Honey? Did Harold teach you and Kathryn Marco's Polo? Does Kathryn hate to put her head under water?"

I am so new to all of this and I have yet to understand. Richard, ever the patient one answers me, "Yes, my love, yes. Everything you tell me from your vision is true."

The next morning Richard is leaving for work. I watch in envy as he walks out the door. I know that I cannot leave the bedroom, much less walk. As I hear Richard's truck start up with a roar and drive down the street, I begin to smile. I think to myself, 'Well, that's all right. I do have something special to look forward to.'

I know that when sleep comes I will be in the presence of Angels. With that thought, and another pain pill, I roll into the pillow and pull the covers over my head. After a few dreams, my visions begin again.

"Honey, I'm home," Richard announces his arrival as he puts his head in the bedroom door.

"I am going to put the groceries away. I'll be right back." When I wake up, I am excited about the dream I just had. Richard makes dinner, delivers it with a flourish, and asks, "So tell me who came to visit you today, Hon?"

CHAPTER 4 I SHARE MY ANGELS

I have always talked in my sleep. I believe it must run in the family. Daniel Dykstra, my youngest brother, sleeps with his eyes half open and mumbles aloud during a few light snores. When my dad, Melvin Dykstra, broke his back and I stayed with him in the hospital, Dad would talk to me as if he were awake. However, I knew my dad must be sleep talking because it was almost midnight.

Somehow, my oldest brother, Terry, and my only sister, Becky, are not affected; I decided they must take after my mom, Jeneane Dykstra,'s side of the family. In school after sleepovers, my friends would make fun of me and even I found it silly. After my surgery, however, Richard and I found a way to use my sleep talking as a gift.

I tell Richard about all the visions I see. Like all dreams, they are fleeting and I cannot remember all the details. Richard is frustrated and begins to search for a way to participate in my visions. One night while hearing me talk in my sleep Richard decided to ask me what I see in my dream.

To Richard's amazement, I answer him about my vision. Richard asks me what I am doing and I respond, "I am under the rainbow playing with the Leprechauns. I am in Hawaii playing in a cove with your mom, your dad, and your grandfather." I begin to name all Richard's family: his aunts, uncles, grandparents, cousins, and even his beloved dog.

When Richard wants to know everyone's age, I ask his family this question. Richard's loved ones respond by telling me their exact birthdays and where they were born. I repeat this information to Richard. Richard was already certain that I had seen his dad during my surgery. Now Richard is convinced that the Angels in my dreams are his family.

Richard keeps asking me for specific details about dates and events that only his family that has passed could have known. He was doing this because he wanted to prove to me and to his brother, Robert Kilmer Moe, that this was real. Over the course of the next six months, Richard wrote numerous emails to his family, confirming all the factual details in my visions.

Richard decided it was important to him to relax and enjoy this gift. He already knew in his heart that these stories were for real but it would take eighteen months for Richard to convince me.

I keep asking Richard, "Are you sure you are not telling me these things before you turn on the recorder? Did this really happen in your past the way I tell the story?"

Richard responds with a sigh and says, "I never told you what perfume my mom wore. I never told you that she wore *'White Shoulders'*."

Richard uses his fingers and continues to tick off items one by one that I have shared with him from my visions.

"Jane, you know all the names of everyone in my family. You told me the story of picking out my puppy and then reminded me of how this puppy threw up on my lap in the International Truck on the way home from buying him."

"You knew the story about me pulling my sister around in the red wagon and selling vegetables and you even knew the candy we bought. How could you have known any of this as well as my sister's addiction to chocolate?"

"Jane, you described my dad in his shop and the tools he made. You even described my home with the swimming pool on Vose Street with the tool shop in the front."

"You told me the story of my Uncle Harold teaching me and Kathryn how to play Marco's Polo and how Kathryn didn't put her head under water."

"You have described my dad in his 'work apron,' how his shoes were not tied up, and the silver things he was making."

"You have described Mom's greenhouse and the wood bench inside."

"You told me about how I made gingerbread houses with my mom and how much I liked to help."

"You told me about all the Christmas' and holidays and how special they are to my mom and how much she loves to do all the decorations."

"You told me about Grandpa Moe getting an award."

"You told me the story about how I got lost in the forest and about the time I got sprayed by a skunk."

"You described all my camping trips, dad's rock, and how we went fishing off of his rock."

"You described the tree before the rock, the tunnel from across the street, and the Leo Carrillo campgrounds."

"You described my sister building sand castles, Dad and I fishing, and Bob surfing at Leo Carrillo."

"You described how Mom regrets not going with us on Sundays."

"You told me that my dad corrected me regarding the age he was when he died; that he was forty-six years old and not forty-five, and you were right."

"You helped me find Dad's grave with no problem. You walked right to it after dreaming about where it was. I couldn't find it when I looked for it."

"You told me that my dad has never let go and how he said he is always the wind in my hair."

"You knew that it took my mom a long time to die and how she hung on because I just couldn't let her go. You even describe how Kathryn and I set her ashes free and where."

"You told me about the night I drove too fast on my motorcycle after drinking a lot of alcohol. I was in my early twenties and no one else was there but me, yet you knew about that night. And you shared with me how Dad is glad my motorcycle is gone because it was so dangerous."

"You told me about the little train station I had, the little turtles I loved, and the time the police brought me home because I was playing with coins on the train tracks."

"You described the way my family looks when you have never seen them before."

"You describe the exact location of the waterfalls in Hawaii where Dad swam as a child, and then you take me there."

"You describe the sailboat, the night Dad was out all night on it, and how my ornery Grandma said, 'I told you he would be okay.'"

"You described the way I used to play tetherball."

"You told me about the time Dad took me to school to show my class how to tie ropes, and how he was so touched that I was proud of him."

"You described my running away from Kindergarten and taking my buddies with me."

"You described Kathryn and her chocolate, my mom and her greenhouse and Orchids, and how Kathryn had Orchids in her bathroom, even before you went there."

Richard looks at me intently and continues, "Now, I rest my case! You have never met my dearly departed yet you have shared stories with me that are a part of our past. There is no way you could know such rich details unless you were with my family and they told you these stories."

I give in but I insist he write emails to his brother and confirm facts for me. With a sigh, Richard reluctantly agrees to write his brother. Over the course of the next year, Richard astonishes me by showing the emails between himself and his older brother, Robert, confirming the details from my vision.

One day I have a question from one of my visions, "Richard, did you know that your Grandpa and Grandma Moe had a servant?" I continue, "Her name was Violet Ishamura."

Richard frowns at me and says, "A servant? There are no servants in the United States."

I rub my head and thinking aloud I respond, "Well, that was Hawaii so who knows?"

Remaining unconvinced Richard researches my latest announcement on the Internet. Lo and behold he finds a nineteen thirty United States Census that lists his grandparents, their children, their mother-in-law, Mary Lane, and guess who; a servant named Violet Ishamura. My doubts begin to unravel. I listen as God tells me to believe. I relax and begin to enjoy my new gift.

Because of the richness in detail and the stories that began to unfold beginning with his conception, Richard continues to record these sessions. Richard does not want to miss any details and is afraid of recording over his beloved stories so he keeps buying new recorders. Richard continues to do this even after five years.

I visit Richard's family in Heaven every night, several times a night. My visits there are exciting and my dreams remain incredible. I dream of Richard's family and pets that have passed on, of my own family, of St. Peter, the beautiful Mother Mary, and of course; I dream of our beloved Jesus. God is there, beautiful and brilliant, a vision to behold within His majestic light.

CHAPTER 5 A GIFT FROM THE ANGELS

Richard has gotten used to my sleep talking after being together for so long. I had nightmares and Richard experienced them first hand from my dreams. Richard always answers me as if he is in my nightmare, chases the bad people away, and makes me feel safe. After my visions began, the Angels saw the nightmares, removed them with ease, and disposed of them in the trash.

From this, Richard knows how to reach into my dreams. He begins a conversation with me while I am sleeping by asking, "What is it?"

If I am having a vision with our loved ones, I will respond to Richard with an answer according to that particular dream.

I always begin my "journey" to Heaven within a tunnel and at the end of this tunnel is a very bright light. This light is brilliant and contains so much love that I cannot wait to step inside. However, before I can enter this light I have to cross what I call 'the

45

whoosh'. I call it this because of the 'whoosh' sound it makes as I cross it. On the other side of this 'whoosh' is a tree, which slants downwards, and helps shield my landing onto a large rock.

Waiting for me on the rock is always Richard's beloved dog, Barney. God has blessed us by allowing our pets to join us in eternity. How wonderful it is to know every living creature, be it treasured pet, the flowers that bloom, or the bees that no longer want to sting, journey with us into a reunion with God.

Barney, "The Barn" has always had this incredible sixth sense about those he loves. Now that we are friends, Barney loves me. In return, I have grown to love Barney from my many trips to his Heaven. Barney knows when I am coming even before I do. He announces my arrival by jumping up and down, up and down, on the rock wiggling with excitement. Barney is never alone while he waits for me to cross the 'whoosh', waiting with him are one or more members from Richard's family.

Today I respond with a dreamy voice, "It's the light but not just any light; it is the most majestic light you will ever see."

Richard turns on his recorder with excitement and says, "What do you see?"

I describe the tunnel, this rock, and a tree before it that glides me gently onto the rock and my journey to Richard. He gushes, "I know that rock and I know that tunnel!"

Richard waits. He does not want to stop me from my vision and holds the rest of his thoughts until after I wake up.

"That rock and that tunnel," Richard jars me from my drowsiness as he continues, "they are from my childhood."

Elated, Richard jumps off the bed and begins to pace. Turning back to me Richard adds excitedly, "My dad used to take us to Leo Carrillo's beach where we would go fishing off that very rock, Kathryn would make sand castles, and Robert would surf."

Richard smiles as he recalls these wonderful memories from his childhood and he continues by sharing them with me, "Jane; we went camping on the other side of that tunnel you are describing."

Richard's eyes are dancing and he is rubbing his face with his hands. Least he goes overboard, Richard rubs his face in this manner as a way of containing himself.

Closing his eyes Richard visualizes his past and continues to share it with me; "My mom and dad would take our family to Leo Carrillo's campground. They used to take us camping every weekend and we went to Leo Carrillo a lot."

Richard opens his eyes as he continues; "Robert, Kathryn, and I loved it there. Mom and Dad knew it was safe and we could go through the campgrounds, take the tunnel under the street, and cross to the Pacific Ocean on the other side."

I begin to share in Richard's excitement and I ask him, "Richard, do you think this weekend you could take me there? I want to see if my vision looks like Leo Carrillo."

Richard leans over and gives me a hug, "I was just thinking the same thing."

Wrinkling his forehead, Richard looks at me intently with those cute hazel eyes and says, "Let's leave early Saturday. I can't wait."

The next weekend Richard and I arrive at Leo Carrillo State Beach. Pushing me in the wheelchair, we arrive breathlessly at Richard's past. I look down at the Pacific Ocean and begin to cry.

Taking Richard's hand in mine I whisper, "Honey, this is it. That is the exact rock from my visions. Richard, do you see above the rock? Do you see the tree right there? That tree is my landing tree. The tree grows in a slanted shape and it helps me land on the rock after the 'whoosh'!"

Looking up Richard answers me, "Yes, I never noticed it before but yes, there is a tree right above the rock."

Touching my cheek, Richard looks at me with a question in his eyes. I know what he is thinking and I set him free, "Go down to the rock, Richard. Have a long talk with your family."

With tears in his eyes, Richard turns and makes his way across the sand and climbs onto the rock from his past. Sitting down by the Pacific Ocean, we both grow quiet as we reflect on our own thoughts, secure in the knowledge that our loved ones have never let go.

The Rock From 'The Whoosh' & Leo Carrillo

VISION 1 THE 'WHOOSH'

The following is a transcript from the recording of a vision I shared with Richard. I am describing how I cross into Heaven via 'the whoosh'.

Jane: If you want to cross the 'whoosh', you go through the tunnel. Can you see that white light up there, the bright light?

Richard: Yes, I see the bright light.

Jane: After you see the bright light, you will see all the Stars, the Sun, the Moon, and you see the Rainbows. After you go up that way, you come to the part that says, 'whoosh'. Once you get across the 'whoosh', you can land on the rock. You have to make your legs long so you can jump over the 'whoosh'.

Richard: I understand.

Jane: The 'whoosh' part wants to keep you here. The other part wants to keep you there. You have to step across the 'whoosh' part. The 'whoosh' part goes 'whoosh', like that. After you step over the 'whoosh' part, you can go up to the white light.

Richard: I have to step over it.

Jane: Yes.

Richard: I understand.

Jane: Then you can go to the glass. You close your eyes right before the glass where the Barn is dancing around on the other side.

Richard: Okay.

Jane: You close your eyes, you think about the rock, and there you are, right there. Once you are there then Mom and Dad can pick you up.

Richard: I will keep working on it.

Jane: Yes. The hard part is the 'whoosh'.

Richard: The hard part is the 'whoosh'?

Jane: Yes.

Richard: I understand.

Jane: I just do not know how to tell you to step across the 'whoosh'.

Richard: Yes. That is the hard part.

Jane: Once you can step across the 'whoosh', the rest of it is easy.

Richard: All right, I will keep working on it.

Jane: It is a little tiring though, the 'whoosh' part.

Richard: Yes.

Jane: It does not have any control. You have the control. Mom says you have to get across the 'whoosh'.

Richard: Okay, I understand.

Jane: It goes 'whoosh', 'whoosh', like that.

Richard: I will keep trying.

Jane: Do not step into it. You step over it.

PART II BEFORE THEY WERE ANGELS

Mable Lane Moe   Kilmer Jr., Kilmer Sr.,
                        Harold, & Lawrence Moe

CHAPTER 6 KILMER SR. & MABLE

Kilmer Oscar Moe Sr. stood proudly at the podium and looked out at the crowd. As Superintendent of the Kamehameha Boy's school in Honolulu, Hawaii, Kilmer Sr. took this podium often: making announcements, observing holidays, and handing out diplomas to his graduates.

To Kilmer Sr. today's event was truly special. Today he was receiving an award for his appointment as

55

President of the Parent Teachers Association for the Islands of Hawaii. Kilmer Sr. felt honored at receiving this title and he was excited, yet nervous about what he was going to say. He was so excited; in fact, that he forgot to bring his notes for this acceptance speech. Kilmer Sr. found he had no choice but to wing it.

Taking a deep breath Kilmer Sr. plunged ahead, speaking slowly and deliberately as was his manner, "I would like to share with this most gracious crowd how honored I am to have been nominated for this award."

Kilmer Sr. turned to the other nominees in his field seated to his left and gave them a slight bow as he continued, "These men and women are all winners in my heart, and I feel humbled to be in their presence."

Kilmer Sr. thanked the teachers for his award and he shared with the crowded room that teaching is not just his vocation; teaching is his passion. Kilmer Sr.'s voice is full of emotion as he tells the crowd that he has wanted to share life and all the wonders it held with students of his own since he was a little boy.

Smiling at the crowd Kilmer Sr. tells his audience the challenges he has met and overcome as an educator since his arrival in Hawaii. Kilmer Sr. began his career in Oahu, Hawaii, as a teacher and after a brief period, Kilmer Sr. accepted a position as Assistant Superintendent. Recently, Kilmer Oscar Moe Sr. received a promotion to his current position and one he treasures, Superintendent of the Kamehameha Boy's School.

Life had not always been this easy for Kilmer Sr. so he never took anything for granted. In February 1882, in La Crosse, Wisconsin, Kilmer Sr. became the third of nine children born to Andrew and Sophia Moe. The oldest was Julius, who was born in 1879. The couple's first Daughter, Bertina, was born in 1881. After Kilmer Sr., Maurice was born in 1884, and then Elmer, born in 1887. The next child born to Andrew and Sophia was Selma, born in 1889, then Ella, in 1891, and Clarence Andrew, in 1894. Baby Ester became the last child born to Andrew and Sophie Moe, in 1898.

Kilmer Sr. became a hardworking, driven man who was as soft and gentle on the inside as he was tough, yet direct on the outside.

A family man, Kilmer Sr. is the proud father of three children: Kilmer Oscar Moe Jr., born October 11, 1923, Harold Gulbert Moe, born January 24, 1925, and Lillian Grace (a.k.a. Lillian Special) Moe, born June 25, 1926. They did not know it yet but Kilmer Sr. and Mable were to have one more child, another Son, born January 5, 1928, whom they would call Lawrence Arthur Moe.

Kilmer Sr. continues to deliver his acceptance speech as he struggles to remember what he had written in his notes. After a while he smiled inwardly and relaxed thinking to himself, 'Self, why I'm doing all right without my notes.'

Finding it was time to sum up his pleasure for today's honor, Kilmer Sr. turns to his family members seated to his right. He takes off his hat and with a twinkle in his eyes says, "I would like to thank my family for their love and support. I could not have won this award without them."

Kilmer Sr. smiles at his children as he continues, "My oldest son, Kilmer Jr., my youngest son, Harold, and my daughter, Lillian, are all with me today. My family brings me so much joy and happiness. I want them to know how very much they mean to me."

Kilmer Sr. wraps up his acceptance speech by announcing, "I love my family very much, and with God's ever generosity I hope to be blessed with more children."

Kilmer Sr. leaves the podium and walks toward his family. He could see his sons and his daughter grinning at him and he smiles back. He looks at his wife, Mable Lane Moe, and begins to wink at her.

Kilmer Sr. wrinkles his forehead as he realizes Mable is frowning at him. Feeling confused, Kilmer Sr. rubs his chin and wonders silently, 'What could be wrong with my wife?'

He would have his answer soon enough. Mable marches up to her husband and with a pinch to his cheek, informs Kilmer Sr. he had not even mentioned her by name.

Kilmer Sr. laughs nervously believing by mistake that he had, "Mable, you are my heart," he says as he tries to reassure Mable that he had. Mable is not convinced, however. She grabs his children by their hands, and marches Junior, Harold, and Lillian out the door. Kilmer Sr., shaking his head with bewilderment, follows his family to the car.

Kilmer Sr. has good reason to be nervous about forgetting to mention his wife. Mable Lane Moe loves her man but she is not a meek, stay in the background, kind of wife.

Born April 12, 1893, Mable Lane Moe has an ornery streak and is quite proud of it. Although the streak of hers pushes Mable helter-skelter through life, Mable is a kind and giving woman. Mable is a wonderful mother to her children and a challenging, yet loving wife to her husband. Mable later becomes a great mother-in-law to Marjorie Powers Moe, the future spouse of Mable's Son, Kilmer Jr.

Mable could charm the buttons off a shirt and everyone who takes the time to know Mable, loves her. Self-described as fiercely independent, Mable is never one to hold her tongue; you always knew exactly what she was thinking. Mable carries her personality on her sleeve and if you ever met her mother, Mary Lane, you knew at once, whom Mable takes after.

Mable likes to share a story about her Mother in which she recalls how her Father got drunk one night and gambled their horses away. Mary Lane found out about it and marched over to the man who had won the prize. The man took one look at Mary Lane and without saying a word, handed her horses over.

Mable liked to say, "Now, what does that tell you about my mom?"

Mable met Kilmer Sr. in the Philippines. Mable fell in love with him right away, perhaps because Kilmer Sr. was her complete opposite. Mable Lane found Kilmer Moe Sr. strong, yet gentle, soft-spoken, quiet, and extremely dependable.

After a short courtship, Kilmer Sr. fell in love with Mable Lane. Although he was quiet, Kilmer Sr. was indeed Mable's match. When the two met in the Philippines' school system, Kilmer Sr. was Mable's boss.

Mable remembers her honeymoon well. In Mable's own words, she describes the time they went horseback riding two days after their wedding and how her horse almost fell off the side of a cliff. To keep her horse and herself safe, Mable threw her weight towards the mountainside, away from the cliff. She leaned her horse so far that at one point both Mable and the horse fell off into the puddles that had formed from the day's rain.

Looking over at Kilmer Sr. Mable fumed and thought, 'He better not laugh at me!'

Mable's new husband was a smart man, however. Although he saw what was happening, Kilmer Oscar Moe Sr. never cracked a grin.

A handsome couple Mable and Kilmer Moe Sr. worked side by side to achieve common goals. When they tired of the Philippines Mable and Kilmer Sr. made their way to Hawaii. Upon their arrival in Honolulu, Mable took one look at the lush paradise and announced she had found her own Heaven. Kilmer Sr. could not agree more.

When Kilmer Sr. and Mable's first child, a Son, was born in Manila, Philippines, it was with pride that Kilmer Sr. gave his first born his name. Kilmer Oscar Moe Jr., was nicknamed Junior. Junior carried this title until the age of ten. Junior not only loves his daddy; he adores him. Kilmer Sr. doted on his son and took him everywhere.

The family lived in a house provided by the Philippine school facility so neither parent had far to go to reach their place of employment. Kilmer Sr. worked across the street from their house in the Administration Building, and Mable taught in the classrooms on the same street; both parents could walk to work. As a toddler, Junior would hold his daddy's hand and walk him, and sometimes his mommy, to the end of their driveway when it was time for one or both to leave for work. While Kilmer Sr. worked full-time after Junior was born, Mable found she wanted to spend more time with her new son. Mable decided to work part-time.

Kilmer Sr. would swoop down, give Junior a hug, and kiss his son good-bye. Locking the gate carefully behind him, Kilmer Sr. stepped onto the sidewalk. With a wave, his daddy would disappear from Junior's view.

Returning home every evening Kilmer Sr. would always find his 'pride and joy' sitting at the gate waiting for him. This was Father and Son's special time and they both loved it.

Violet Ishamura became their servant. In the Philippines and Hawaii during this period, servants worked for their sponsors in return for immigration to the United States. However, 'servant' is not an appropriate title for Violet Ishamura. Violet became part of the family and she not only loves the children as if they are her own, Violet helped to raise them as well.

Violet watches the 'little tyke' while Mable is away. Violet is already outdoors with Junior when Mable would come home from work. As was her habit Mable kisses her son, sits down on the front porch, and grades papers from the day.

Mable smiles as she watches Junior play near the front gate. Junior knew when it was time for his beloved daddy to come home and he would not play anywhere else. Both Mable and Violet Ishamura know that Junior is waiting for his best friend to come home and will not move from his post. Mable and Violet did not even try.

With delight, Junior would announce his daddy's arrival by shouting, "Daddy, Daddy, Daddy!" After Kilmer Sr. would unlock the gate, Junior would jump into his daddy's waiting arms. Off they would go together, Kilmer Sr. swinging his beloved son around and around. Ruffling his hair Kilmer Sr. would ask Junior about his day and tell his first-born how much he had missed him.

Junior was an extremely intelligent child with a photographic memory. With pride, Kilmer Sr. taught his son everything he knew. It was a magical childhood for Junior and he hung on to his daddy's every word, absorbing everything. Junior would carry these lessons all of his life.

Kilmer Sr. was a good hunter and an even better angler. He loved both sports and as his son matured, Kilmer Sr. would take Junior along. Always the teacher, Kilmer Sr. would explain to his son everything he was doing while he was doing it.

Junior grew up knowing the names of every fish they caught, which hook was used to catch that fish, and why. Kilmer Sr. would explain to his son the reasons behind everything he did.

Kilmer Sr. and his son also shared a love of the Ocean. Holding his young son close, Kilmer Sr. would put Junior on top of his surfboard and they would ride a small wave together as it rushed towards the shore.

Junior took to the water like a fish and swam through the waves as if it presented no challenge to him. Bobbing through the surf Junior looked like a dolphin as he propelled himself through the Pacific Ocean.

When Junior got older, his daddy surprised him with his very own surfboard. Father and son loved to race towards the beach and then try to out-surf each other. Junior made his daddy smile when his brothers and his sister came along; Junior taught them to love the Pacific Ocean as much as he does.

Harold Gulbert Moe is the second child born to Mable and Kilmer Sr. Like Junior; Harold was also born in the Philippines. Harold would one-day serve in the Army, meet the love of his life (the beautiful Betty Sue), and settle down in Reynoldsburg, Ohio, where Harold would form his own Engineering firm. Harold and Betty Sue have three children: David, Laura, and Paul. David is married to his lovely wife, Donnas, and they present Harold and Betty Sue with three beautiful Grandchildren, Heather Charlotte (Moe) Blain, Erica Lynn (Moe) Hodges, and Jeffrey Christer Moe. Laura lives in Ohio and is a High School teacher. Sadly, Paul perishes with his dad, Harold, in a fire at their home in Ohio.

Lillian (a.k.a. Special) Grace Moe is Junior's only sister. Kilmer Jr. became very close after a sailboat accident; the sailboat sweeps Kilmer Jr. out to sea. Lillian nurses both her dad and her big brother back to health after the elements take their toll one dreadful night.

Lillian and Kilmer Jr. remain close to this day and Kilmer Jr. takes very good care of his little sister. Lillian accidentally took an overdose when she was in her twenties. Lillian received electric shock treatment while in the hospital trying to recover. This dosage was not diagnosed correctly and subsequently fried her brain. Lillian lived in a mental institution the rest of her life, through no fault of her own, chained to her bed.

In Heaven Lillian chooses to be the beautiful 'childlike' girl she was before the accident. Lillian spends the rest of her life in Heaven with her beloved big brother, Kilmer Jr., their mom and dad, and Marjorie, Kilmer Jr.'s wife.

Lawrence, the baby of the family, ran away at age seventeen to join the Merchant Marines. Lawrence does so against his parent's wishes because he was angry with his Mother. Mable refused to let Lawrence buy a convertible car that he wanted. Knowing that these cars can be dangerous, Mable wants to keep her son safe. Lawrence disappears and he never contacts his family again.

Summers in Hawaii are magical; they brought out the creative side of Kilmer Sr. and Kilmer Jr. Every summer Father and Son would pick a new project to complete together, one that they could work on as a team. One summer Kilmer Jr. and Kilmer Sr. decided it was time to make a new sailboat. They work hard into the nights, taking the whole summer to complete their project. When it was finished, Junior is a 'young tyke' at the age of ten. Junior seems very mature as he looks up at his daddy and begs him to launch their project by himself. Kilmer Sr. knows his son has a great deal of experience with sailboats, so with a smile Kilmer Sr. grants his son's request.

It was a beautiful, balmy, summer day when Kilmer Sr. takes Junior and their newly built sailboat to the cove by their home for its maiden sail. Junior has christened his new masterpiece 'The Kim' because he now prefers this new nickname. He and his dad set 'The Kim' to sail in the tropical waters of Oahu, Hawaii.

Because of the events that transpire from a storm, this maiden sail becomes an event a loving Father will never forget. This story shares the love between not only a Father and his son; it also reflects the love that exists between the entire Moe families, as well.

Kilmer Sr. & Kilmer Jr. Moe

VISION 2 SWEPT OUT TO SEA

The following recording is a typed transcript from my vision about the night Richard's Dad, Kilmer Oscar Moe Jr., took his new sailboat out for its maiden sail. Richard's Dad and Richard's paternal Grandfather, Kilmer Oscar Moe Sr., are both telling me this story. Richard, reaching into my dreams, speaks to me as I sleep. In this transcript, I refer to Kilmer Oscar Moe Jr. as either 'your dad' or 'Dad,' and Kilmer Oscar Moe Sr.; I refer to as 'Grandpa.' 'Mom' in this story is Richard's Mother, Marjorie Jane Powers Moe, and 'Grandma' is Richard's paternal Grandmother, Mable Lane Moe.

I am dreaming and Richard reaches into my vision.

Richard: Can I ask Dad a story?

67

Jane: I can ask him but Dad can hear you.

Richard: Dad, could I hear the story about when you got lost on the sailboat, the one when the sailboat broke?

Jane: Yes. (Long pause while I listen to Richard's Dad and Richard's Grandpa Moe as they both recall the incident and I see the past in my vision). It is quite a long story. Dad is going to tell me a little bit right now.

Richard: I know. We do not want you to get too tired.

Jane: Dad was not lost.

Richard: No, I know. Dad was not lost.

Jane: Do you mean the time when Dad was in the storm?

Richard: Hmm, I think he was gone all night in the storm. Yes, I would like to hear that one.

Jane: The boat Dad was on was a sailboat. Dad was just sailing, and sailing, and sailing. He was having so much fun on the sailboat, the first one that your dad and his daddy (Grandpa Moe) had made together for your dad.

Richard: Is that right?

Jane: Well, that's what Dad says. Dad was trying to make it just right. His daddy was helping him make it, too.

Richard: I understand.

Jane: Is that the story you want? Is that what you are asking about because he has so many?

Richard: Well, yes.

Jane: The long one is about the storm.

Richard: You know let's do the story about my dad making the sailboat with his dad, Kilmer Sr. You can tell the other one when you are not so tired.

Jane: Dad and Grandpa are making the sailboat. He was so happy. Then Dad and Grandpa took your dad out for the sailboat's maiden sail. Dad was trying to sail here and there. He was so happy because he loves to sail. Grandpa was by the water on a pier and he is watching his son from there.

Grandpa says, 'Pull it to the stern, Son. Pull it to the stern.' Dad could not hear Grandpa because a storm was coming. Grandpa could not hear your dad.

Dad is looking at Grandpa and trying to tell his dad that the boat is starting to come apart underneath his feet. Dad did not know what to do. Dad is looking at Grandpa. His daddy is getting further and further away.

The wind is blowing him away from his daddy. Grandpa is telling Dad something that your dad cannot hear. Dad is trying to hear Grandpa but he is more worried about what is happening underneath the boat. The sailboat part is coming apart. Dad does not know why it is doing that. Dad is thinking of smart things to do.

Dad takes his belt off. He ties it around the pieces that are coming apart. It is not holding it together because Dad does not wear a real belt. He wears a rope belt. Dad is looking at Grandpa. He cannot see Grandpa any more. The rain is coming and the wind is blowing all around. Is this the story you want?

Richard: Yes.

Jane: Dad starts to think, 'What would my daddy do?' Dad does not know what to do. Dad is just a 'young tyke' and he is thinking about all the stories Grandpa told him all his lifetime. Grandpa told him stories all the time; when they would go hunting, when they would go fishing, when they go making stuff. His daddy always told him stories.

Richard: Is that right?

Jane: Dad is thinking, 'What would my daddy do? If it were my daddy, what would he do?' Then Dad realized that the sail parts, the part that sails you around and around....

Richard: Okay.

Jane: Is very strong stuff... Huh? It is very strong materials.

Richard: Yes.

Jane: It was made of very strong material stuff. No. I am not too tired, Dad. I will just tell him this part. Dad always has a Boy Scout knife in his pocket.

Richard: I understand.

Jane: Grandpa gave him the knife.

Richard: Wow!

Jane: It is special to Dad so he reached in his pocket...There is a whole bunch more to the story but Dad is telling me the short stuff.

Richard: Yes. You are tired and we do not want you to be too tired.

Jane: Dad pulled out this knife. He cuts down the strong materials.

Richard: I understand.

Jane: Dad tied that around the boat part and around the bottom part, the part that is coming apart.

Richard: Yes.

Jane: Yes, then Dad uses his rope belt and he ties those materials together. It is holding everything together. Dad saw it and he is holding on to the boat because the wind is blowing him...Huh? Okay, the wave is blowing him...Huh? Okay, Dad, the waves are tossing him this way and tossing him that way, tossing him this way and tossing him that way. Dad is holding on for dear life.

Dad feels like it is going to buck him off so he is just holding on. The waves are getting bigger and bigger and he says to himself, 'Self, why I could probably surf home,' but Dad does not know which way is home. Dad does not want me to tell you this. He was scared.

Richard: It was a learning experience.

Jane: Your mom is getting upset because she did not know the story. She did not know that it was so dangerous. Dad is holding on and holding on. This is Hawaii and in Hawaii why, the weather can change just like that. Before Dad knows it, it is calming down. The water is changing around him and Dad could see the beginning of the cove but he could not swim that far. Dad could not sail because he used the strong materials to hold the boat together.

Richard: I understand.

Jane: So he thinks, 'What would my daddy do?' Your dad knows he cannot swim that far and he cannot get the boat to go that far with his little arms because he is just a young man, so Dad takes off his pants. It is... (Jane is chuckling). It is not his underpants, Mom, just the big pants. He tied them around the top.

Richard: I understand.

Jane: Dad makes himself a sailboat by tying the hole from the leggy parts of his pants.

Richard: Wow!

Jane: Dad is going, and he is going, and he is going, and he is swimming a little bit with his little arms, going a little bit in the right direction. Grandpa has been out there all night long in the storm, watching, wringing his hands, yelling for his son, and crying. He will not leave the site, the site where he saw his son the last time.

When Grandpa sees Dad, (Jane crying) he is so happy. (Jane continues to cry). He is so happy. Grandpa sees his son and he sees the pants as a sailboat.

Richard: Wow!

Jane: Grandpa is swimming out there to save your dad and his son is so very thirsty, hungry, and tired.

Richard: Yes.

Jane: Dad started slipping off the side of the boat. Grandpa catches his son.

Richard: Is that right?

Jane: Grandpa takes his son back to the side of the waters. Grandpa says, 'Don't you ever scare me like that again, Son.'

Dad says, 'Get my sailboat, Daddy. Get my sailboat.'

Richard laughs.

Jane: Grandpa he's a little bit mad and he is saying, 'Oh, brother.'

Richard chuckles.

Jane: Grandpa goes out there and he grabs that sailboat and he is somewhat mad at it at first, then he realizes....I know that part, Dad. Grandpa realizes that it saved his son's life so they keep that sailboat forever and ever. That is the short part of the story there is some more. Your dad was sick for a couple of days. He had a very high fever.

Richard: Is that right?

Jane: Yes. Dad was very sick from that.

Richard: Is that right?

Jane: That is the story that you want?

Richard: Yes, Dad, thank you. That is quite a story.

Jane: Dad was quite an adventurous....

Richard: Yes.

Jane: He was quite an adventurous guy. Dad got in trouble sometimes.

Richard: I see.

Jane: weeping, Grandpa, he loves your dad so much. Everybody is crying.

Richard: Yeah, but if something bad had happened he would not have been my daddy.

Jane: He would not have met your mom, either.

Richard: I know.

VISION 3 LILLIAN IS A SPECIAL GIRL

The following recorded vision takes place after Richard's Dad, Kilmer Oscar Moe Jr., and Richard's paternal Grandfather, Kilmer Oscar Moe Sr., became ill from the 'Swept Out To Sea' incident. Lillian is the only sister of Kilmer Oscar Moe Jr. and she nurses both her dad and her brother back to health. Kilmer Oscar Moe Sr., I refer to as 'Grandpa,' and Richard's paternal Grandmother, Mable Lane Moe, I refer to as 'Grandma' or 'the ornery Grandma.'

Jane: Lillian, she was just a little girl. Grandma was pacing back and forth and back and forth on the front porch. The ornery Grandma says, 'Oh, he'll be okay,' like that. Lillian could see that they were sick and she is trying to make them soup on the Potbelly stove. She was just a little girl making the soup. The soup was coming out pretty good. She would put the soup down her big brother's mouth. Every time he opens his mouth to say something, down goes the soup. Lillian did the same thing with her dad; your Grandpa Moe. When Grandpa would start snoring (snore, snore) then

Lillian would pour the soup into his mouth. Then Lillian puts some more water down both of their mouths. She is taking good care of both her dad and her brother.

Richard: I understand.

Jane: Yes, Lillian makes them better.

Richard: She did?

Jane: Yes. Lillian made the soup on that old Potbelly stove that they had. She mopped up their foreheads, she changed their clothes, and she tried to change their bed. She could not change the bed because it was too heavy.

Richard: I see. Good job, Lillian.

Jane: This occasion is when her big brother and Lillian became close and the best of friends. She would sit by the bed and hold their hands.

Richard: Is that right?

Jane: Yes.

Richard: I see. That is a sweet story.

Jane: Lillian is telling you that part.

Richard: Yes, thanks, Lillian. Thank you for taking care of your big brother.

Jane: Thanks for taking care of Grandpa, too!

Richard: Thanks, Lillian, for taking care of Grandpa. You're our special girl.

Kilmer Oscar Moe Sr.

VISION 4 HE THINKS HE'S SANTA

The following vision is a story retold by Kilmer Oscar Moe Sr., Richard's paternal Grandfather, whom I refer to as 'Grandpa' or 'Grandpa Moe.' Lillian is the Daughter of Kilmer Oscar Moe Sr. and Mable Lane Moe, Richard's paternal Grandmother, whom I refer to as 'Mable.' Lawrence is the youngest Son of Kilmer Oscar Moe Sr. and Mable Lane Moe. The other children I am referring to are their other sons, Harold Gulbert Moe and Kilmer Oscar Moe Jr.

　　Jane: Grandpa is telling me a Christmas story.
　　Richard: He is telling a Christmas story?

Jane: Yes, Grandpa Moe is telling me a Christmas story.

Richard: Really?

Jane: They want to be careful so little children do not hear. Little children do not know the truth about Santa. There are no little children around right now so it is okay if I repeat this story.

Richard: I understand.

Jane: The Grandpa wanted to surprise his children. Grandpa was coming down the chimney, 'Ho, ho, ho,' like that. Grandpa was trying to convince his children that Santa was real. Grandpa was coming down the chimney and he had toys in his bag. He put stuff around his belly so he could go, 'Ho, ho, ho.' He is coming down the chimney and Grandpa is stuck right in the middle of the chimney. He cannot go up and he cannot go down. Grandpa Moe is stuck.

Jane and Richard both chuckle.

Jane: Mable, she had to pull him down from the chimney. Mable is just a little thing and she got a little bit upset. Mable had to take Grandpa down a little bit at a time and then the children saw him and they knew that he was really Santa Claus.

Richard: I see. They did?

Jane: Yes, I like that story.

Richard: I love that story. I never heard that story before.

Jane: Lillian, she is laughing because she remembers.

Richard: She remembers?

Jane: Yes.

Richard: It is a cute story.

Jane: I can just see Grandpa doing that.

Richard: Yes. Grandpa has a good sense of humor.

Jane: The baby, Lawrence, did not see anything. Therefore, for a year, they still get to pretend as if Santa was real.

Richard: I understand.

Mildred Rupert Powers & Robert Irvin Powers

CHAPTER 7 BELOVED GRANDPARENTS

"Mildred and Robert sitting in a tree, K-I-S-S-I-N-G, first comes love, then comes marriage, then comes Robert pushing the baby carriage."

Mildred Powers would smile when the kids in her lovely Wauwatosa, Wisconsin, neighborhood sang this tune to her. When the weather was good, the kids entertained themselves by jumping rope on the sidewalk that ran down their block.

When they saw Mildred coming home with a bag of groceries, these neighborhood kids would change whatever song they had been chanting and begin to serenade Mildred with hers.

More often than not, Mildred would sit her shopping down, and with a smile, join the kids as she jumped between their twirling ropes. Squealing with delight, the children loved how Mildred would play with them. Humming the tune as she put her groceries away, Mildred chuckled as she realized the song was a reflection of her dreams. Ever since she was a little girl, all she ever wanted was to fall in love, get married, and have babies. Now that she was married to a man she was deeply in love with, Mildred knew her dreams were coming true.

Mildred met the man of her dreams, Robert Irvin Powers, in school; they were high school sweethearts. Robert is an Engineer at Wisconsin Energy Company and Mildred fulfilled her lifelong dream of being a homemaker.

Before they settled down to married life, Robert had bought their new home with a huge picture window in the front and a large yard in the back.

They both wanted enough space in their new home for the children they planned for and this house was almost perfect. The only thing missing was a swing on the front porch; something for which Robert said, he had always had 'a-hankering.' Someday, he decided, they would add one.

One day Mildred heard of a neighbor who was a gifted 'handyman,' and set in motion a little surprise for her cherished husband. After searching for days, Mildred found 'the cutest little swing in all of Milwaukee' and hired the 'handyman' to install the gift.

Robert spotted the new swing as he pulled their Ford into the driveway. The love he felt at that moment for his wife gave him a huge lump in his throat and he had to clear it several times before he stepped out of the car. Mildred, who was waiting for him on the porch with a broad smile, melted into his arms as he swept her up and planted kisses all over her face. He swung her around and they laughed as he placed her next to him on the swing. As they held hands, she put her head on his shoulder and they swung back and forth together well into the night.

When Mildred first heard the doctor deliver the news that she was expecting a baby, Mildred dropped to her knees in prayer. Tears of gratitude were streaming down her cheeks as she thanked the great Lord above for this wonderful gift.

Robert was also excited about the prospect of a 'little one' in the house. Every day he would walk in the door after work, swoop Mildred up into his arms, and with a big hug; stroke her tummy and say, "Well?"

It had only been two months since they had been 'a-tryin' but he just could not help himself. Robert was so in love with this woman. The thought of Mildred bearing his child would cause this loving man's chest to swell with pride.

On this cold February afternoon that Mildred received the good news; Robert came home from work and swept through the front door. Calling her name, Robert walked from room to room looking for his wife. Mildred was nowhere in sight. Robert was surprised because usually Mildred is in the kitchen baking up one of her wonderful dinners. However, today was different.

Robert finally came to the last room down the hall, their bedroom. When he stepped into their love nest, he found his beautiful bride sitting on their bed with the smile of an Angel on her face. Mildred was wearing a new smock and as he swept her off the bed, he caught the scent of a different perfume.

Hugging Mildred, he sat her down so he could study her. Robert enjoyed sharing her efforts after she had gone shopping but he was surprised at today's choice. This new outfit was not her usual style and he did not understand at first. Mildred smiled at him with tears in her eyes and finally he knew the answer. Mildred was wearing a maternity top.

Robert looked into Mildred's eyes and asked without saying a word. He knew the answer he was about to receive so with a smile he played along, "Well?"

Mildred knows how to please her husband and as she pulled his mouth to hers she whispered with love in her voice, "Yes, my Robert, yes. We are pregnant."

Seven months later Robert and Mildred are eagerly awaiting the birth of their first child. On a day they will never forget, Robert went to work with his usual gusto. Mildred is sitting in her rocking chair knitting another pair of booties for the baby; yellow in color because they did not know the sex of their unborn child. Robert and Mildred didn't mind, they prayed for a healthy baby. Mildred and Robert are both excited that the time to deliver their baby has finally arrived.

As Mildred got up to fetch another cup of juice, she felt a sharp stab in her back. A few minutes later, Mildred felt another stab. Mildred thought labor pains would come about in her stomach so she gave these stabs no mind at all. Sitting back down in her favorite chair Mildred chocked it all up to pregnancy and began to knit again.

The pains kept coming through and Mildred could not stand up. Suddenly, Mildred knew. This was no false alarm, 'The baby, oh my; the baby is coming.' Mildred tried to rush to the phone to call her husband but the best she could do was a quick waddle. In a panic, she dialed the wrong number, hung up, and redialed.

Breathlessly, Mildred explained to Robert that she needed him and he was out the door before he realized he had forgotten to hang up the phone. Robert made it home in time to be there for his wife and baby, but just barely.

On September 20, 1925, Marjorie Jane Powers made her entrance into the world as quickly as she would do everything else in her life. Mildred and Robert Powers knew they would never forget that wonderful day they brought Marjorie Jane; swaddled in yellow, home from the hospital. The day was perfect; having dawned with the lushness that those living in the Midwest look forward to all year. All the browns, rusts, and yellows were already making their way into the trees around the Powers home in Wauwatosa, Wisconsin. Robert smiled at the world around him as he tenderly tucked his new daughter into her crib and his exhausted wife into their bed.

A kind, carefree, and easy child, Marjorie Jane Powers brought such joy to her parents. Marjorie loved to race around the house with her daddy as he pretends to be a wild Mustang with Marjorie clinging to his back.

Digging in her heels and squealing with delight Marjorie yells at her daddy, "Faster Daddy, run faster."

Robert's response is a loud neigh and off they go racing around the house again. Laughing, Robert finishes the game with a sigh and delivers Marjorie to her mommy.

Reaching down and scooping Marjorie onto her hip, Mildred looks into the eyes that are so like her own and asked the question her daughter is waiting for, "Marjorie Jane, what shall we bake today?"

Having a four-year olds sense of adventure, Marjorie squirms out of her mom's embrace and scoots off to open Mildred's recipe box. Eyes wide with wonder and smacking her lips with anticipation of the yummiest to come, Marjorie touches each card saying, "Eenie meenie minie moe."

Pulling out one of the cards Marjorie skips back to her mom, points to her card, and says, "What does this card say, Mommy?"

Mildred drops to her knees, studies the index card, and announces, "These are the instructions for making brownies. Does this sound like the winner, Marjorie?"

Marjorie meets her mom's question with smacks of delight. Pulling out the stool she uses to help her mommy in the kitchen, Marjorie climbs up and awaits the spoon and mixing bowl she knows are on their way.

These smacks of anticipation are not just coming from Marjorie, either. Robert has been watching this afternoon routine from his rocking chair in the living room and his mouth begins to water.

Shaking his evening paper open, Robert begins to read as his attention wanders back and forth to the delightful aromas coming from the kitchen. Smiling, Robert turns the pages as he listens to his girls baking in the kitchen. When he hears Marjorie calling to him that they were twirling the frosting, Robert lays his paper down and heads for the brownies.

Mildred and Robert have another Daughter, Rosemary Irene Powers. Rosemary decides later in life, however, that she prefers the name, Rip. Marjorie and

Rosemary play in the snow with their parents, making snowmen and snow angels, and throwing snowballs at each other. Mildred would bundle her girls in matching clothes and they would race around the backyard playing tag. In the summer, the girls loved to climb into their bathing suits and run through the water from their garden hose, laughing and sliding.

Everyone who knew Robert and Mildred Powers, and their well-mannered daughters, came to adore this wonderful family. Robert and Mildred were a kind and giving couple that would go out of their way to help others. Mildred would bake every day and deliver her yummy projects to others in need. She kept an ear open and if Mildred heard someone was sick or had any hardship at all, why she was 'Johnny-on-the-spot' to bring her kitchen to theirs. Sometimes all she could do is just listen and be there but Mildred did not mind. Mildred would say, "To be a true friend to another person, you take the good with the bad, and the ups with the downs. It brings me a great deal of joy to be there when a friend calls out my name."

When it was time for their daughters to marry and have children, Mildred and Robert were overjoyed with their new role. They doted on their grandchildren. They have six in all: three girls and three boys. Two of the boys are the Son's of Marjorie Jane Powers Moe and Kilmer Moe Jr.: Richard Powers Moe and Robert Kilmer Moe. The other Grandson is Johnny, the Son of Rosemary Irene Powers Culver, and her husband, John Culver. Two of their granddaughters are the Daughters of Rosemary and John Culver: Robin and Martha. Kathy Lane Moe is the only Daughter born to Marjorie and Kilmer Moe Jr. In the summer time, Robert and Mildred would invite their grandchildren to come for a spell.

Most of the time, their grandsons were too busy with their buddies to accept a trip for the summer to Grandma and Grandpa's house. However, their granddaughters were delighted at the prospect. Having been to Grandma Millie and Grandpa Bob's home previously, the girls knew what a wonderful vacation was in store for them.

Many summers, Kathy Lane Moe would fly to see her Grandma Millie and Grandpa Bob with her cousin, Robin Culver. Kathy and Robin would excitedly mark the days off their calendars while waiting for the big day to arrive. They couldn't wait to leave for Grandma and Grandpa's house.

Mildred and Robert knew they spoiled their beloved granddaughters when they came, but they did not care. Why, that is what Grandchildren are for as far as they are concerned.

Mildred loved to play games with Kathy and Robin, she even taught them to jump rope. In return, they taught Grandma Millie to play hopscotch. Mildred also loved to bake for her granddaughters. Following the aroma from Mildred's gingerbread cookies cooling on the racks in the windows, Robin and Kathy would race in the house with knowing smiles on their faces. They knew it was time for a snack and Kathy and Robin would open the china closet, pull out the plates and glasses, and head for the refrigerator.

Both girls knew from experience that the best way to eat Grandma Millie's cookies is to dip them into the coldest milk that only the 'milkman' could deliver. Robin and Kathy loved the glass bottles of milk that came to Grandma Millie and Grandpa Bob's house. The girls knew when the 'milkman' had been there because they could see his truck driving down the hill, taking the next delivery to the neighbor. With glee, both girls would run to the porch. It was always a race between the two as they ran back to the kitchen. Who would get those glass bottles of milk to Grandma Millie the fastest?

Mildred knew back then that they did not have fancy toys like those they do nowadays, so she entertained her granddaughters by showing them how to play with paper dolls. Mildred taught her girls that if you were careful and drew inside the lines, why you could color the clothes for the paper dolls, too.

Mildred loved to put those dolls on display. She taught the girls how to make 'May Baskets' and deliver those paper dolls smack in the middle of the baskets. After her girls went home, Mildred would proudly show the finished projects to anyone that would listen.

Robert had to get in on the act, as well. When Grandpa Bob would come home from work, he would tease the girls by rubbing a dandelion under their chins. With childlike innocence, Kathy and Robin would look up at Grandpa Bob as he examined the results of his game. If the dandelion powder came off on their chins Grandpa would announce, "Oh boy, Grandma, look out. Our girls are going to have a boyfriend today."

If the yellow spores did not come off on their chins Grandpa Bob would smile, give them a hug, and say with a laugh, "Sorry, girls, no boyfriends today."

Sunday was the Lord's Day and when Kathy and Robin came in the summer, they would go to church.

Mildred and Robert were proud when they heard from friends how well Kathy and Robin would behave in a place of worship. Their granddaughters would bow their heads and pray, often louder, and with more gusto, than anyone else in the Parish would pray.

For both Kathy and Robin these unforgettable summers passed too quickly. Kathy and Robin come to treasure the amazing vacations they spent with Grandma Millie and Grandpa Bob. Holding these memories deep in their hearts, Kathy and Robin have never forgotten how special Robert and Mildred made these summers, and how much they love their beloved grandparents.

Leaving behind a wonderful legacy, Robert and Mildred Powers are two amazing individuals who gave so much of themselves to everyone they knew.

Robin Culver   Kathy Lane Moe

VISION 5 MAGICAL SUMMERS

The following recording is a vision in which I describe to Richard a visit that Robin Culver and Kathy Moe took one summer to see Robert and Mildred Powers, their beloved maternal Grandparents. Robin and Kathy I refer to by name, 'they,' or as 'the girls.' Grandma Powers is 'Grandma Millie,' 'she,' or 'Grandma.' Richard and I refer to Grandpa Bob as 'he, 'Grandpa,' or 'Robert.'

91

Jane: Kathy and Robin played with the paper dolls at Grandma's house.

Richard: They did?

Jane: Yes. They played with the ones that you take the little wings and you fold them over the shoulders.

Richard: You do?

Jane: Yes. They are paper dolls.

Richard: I see. They are paper dolls.

Jane: They did not have many things to play with back then but you could color the clothes if you wanted to.

Richard: They liked to play with those?

Jane: Yes.

Richard: That is great.

Jane: Grandma showed them how.

Richard: That is great. Do they have any more stories of what they did together?

Jane: She would sing, *"Somewhere Over The Rainbow."*

Richard: Wow.

Jane: She loved that song about the rainbow.

Richard: That is beautiful.

Jane: I know.

Richard: That is a beautiful song. Wow, she loved having the children come to visit, huh?

Jane: Yes, she loved to spoil them.

Richard: Yes?

Jane: She would get them fresh milk. The 'milkman' would come and bring them glass bottles of the milk. She would show them how to go get the milk off the front porch after the 'milkman' had been there. They would have fresh milk. They loved that!

Richard: They did?

Jane: Yes, with the cookies.

Richard: I see.

Jane: They drank the milk with the Gingerbread cookies.

Richard: That's great, Grandma.

Jane: Grandma, not Great-Grandma.

Richard: No, I said Grandma.

Jane: I see, I thought you said Great-Grandma.

Richard: No, I said Grandma. Grandma Powers.

Jane: I understand.

Richard: Grandma, the girls really enjoyed that so much!

Jane: Um hum, that is what she remembers.

Richard: I see. You made the girls very, very happy.

Jane: No, they made her very, very happy.

Richard: Well, they made each other very happy.

Jane: Robert would come home and he would get the dandelions, bring them in, and he would rub them under their chins. If the dandelion would rub off under their chins he would say, 'Oh boy, you're going to find a boyfriend.' If it didn't come off under their chins he would say, 'Nope, not today.'

Richard chuckles.

Jane: The girls would follow him around laughing. They would make 'Mayday Baskets.' They would pick the Violets and the Dandelions and put them in the round little construction cups.

Richard: Wow.

Jane: They did not have many toys back then so they made up things to do. They would put popcorn in the little baskets. They would run around, skip, and say, 'Wee.' They would teach Grandma how to play hopscotch. One, two, pick up that rock right there, skip, skip, one, two, throw the rock. That is how you play hopscotch.

    Richard: Wow!

    Jane: She taught them how to jump rope.

    Richard: Wow, those were special times.

Marjorie Jane Powers   Kilmer Oscar Moe Jr.

CHAPTER 8 MOST BEAUTIFUL ANGEL

The first time Marjorie Jane Powers saw Kilmer Oscar Moe Jr. was at a donut shop near the University of Stout in Menomonie, Wisconsin. Marjorie Jane would go back to the donut shop several times. She wanted to have a conversation with the handsome guy who kept busy frying up the donuts; however, he never looked up from his work. When it did not work out Marjorie Jane moved on and went about the business of attending college.

Marjorie's roommate, Mary, decided it was time for Marjorie to attend an upcoming football game where they both were attending college. Marjorie never cared for the game but Mary adored the sport and her excitement over the upcoming game was contagious. So on this beautiful, crispy, first day of October, Marjorie and Mary showed their team spirit by heading towards the stadium. Chattering away with excitement, they climbed to the top of the bleachers. Mary and Marjorie found two seats together and began cheering for their team. Well, to be honest Mary was the one doing all the cheering. Marjorie did not have a clue what those boys on the field were doing.

Marjorie found herself a little bored and without thinking she began to scan the crowd, but not for long. Marjorie is a good friend and her mind only wandered for a moment. She pulled her eyes back to the field and tried to pay attention to the game.

Glancing at her, Marjorie wondered if Mary knew why those boys were out there on the field beating each other up. She remained silent, however, as was her nature. Giving Mary a hug, Marjorie watched the Cheerleaders on the sidelines as the girls jumped and clapped their hands in unison.

Marjorie has a sweet and caring disposition. She would go out of her way to make everyone happy. In return, Mary loves her roommate and she found she could talk to Marjorie about anything.

'Watching the game is tough on these hard bleachers,' Marjorie thought. She kept these feelings to herself as Mary patiently explained a call from a Referee.

Marjorie found she enjoyed watching the band strut its stuff out on the field and on the sidelines. She closed her eyes and feeling the beat of the drums, hummed along with the music.

In the middle of a note, Marjorie felt a pair of eyes on her so she looked down to see who had distracted her from her diversion.

Kilmer Oscar Moe Jr. has just arrived at the game with his buddies. They were making their way up the bleachers when Kilmer Jr.'s eyes swept past Marjorie, stopped, and returned to stare at her.

As Marjorie looked down the eyes of the, 'most handsome man I have ever seen,' met her eyes. Kilmer Oscar Moe Jr. is looking at her intently but glances away shyly as he realizes she sees him. He smiled to himself and thought, 'Wow, now that is the most beautiful little Angel I have ever seen!' Telling himself not to look again so she would not think he was rude, Kilmer Jr. tried to pretend he was scanning the crowd looking for someone.

Putting his hand over his eyes to shield them from the bright lights above the bleachers, Kilmer Jr. tried to appear nonchalant. Kilmer Jr. could not help himself though and after his brief stab at playing hard to get, his eyes came to rest again on Marjorie. Marjorie returned his calm gaze and thought to herself, 'There is the cute guy from the doughnut shop. I wonder if he is looking for me. He is so cute.'

Despite the flutter that she felt in her stomach, Marjorie knew this was a moment unlike any other. She cocked her head and smiled at Kilmer Jr. thinking, 'I hope he goes to this college.'

Kilmer Jr. had no choice but to pull his eyes forward. His buddies were still walking. As he follows, they deliver him into a bleacher several aisles away from Marjorie. They had just found the perfect seat from which to watch the game.

Kilmer Jr. looked out of the corner of his eye. He wanted to recapture the vision of this girl who was melting his heart. As his eyes darted back and forth from the game to this Angel, his mind wandered until he came up with the perfect idea.

Kilmer Moe Jr. headed toward the concession stand. Making his way past his buddies, he turned right instead of left because he wanted to take the long way around. Kilmer Jr. knew if he wanted his idea to work, he would have to walk right in front of where the object of his attention was sitting.

Marjorie Jane's heart is all a flutter. She asks herself, 'How can I meet him?'

Finally, Marjorie turned to Mary and stammered, "Mary, may I have a nickel, please?"

Marjorie did not carry a purse when she went out with her friends. Everyone would make fun of the way she had to have her money just so; with all the bills lined up perfectly and the coins in their proper order. Marjorie's friends would carry her money for her if they were going anywhere for an extended period. They felt it was faster than waiting while Marjorie would rearrange her money, while still in line mind you, until every piece was perfectly in place. Marjorie is a good natured, kind, and giving soul. With a laugh at herself, she would always accept her friend's offer: first to carry her money, then for the all-important task of putting it away.

Mary reaches into her coin purse and delivers the nickel into Marjorie's waiting hands.

Marjorie curls her fingers around the coin as Mary asks, "Where are you going, Marjorie?"

Marjorie throws her ponytail over her shoulder and with a tug on her white poodle skirt replies, "I am a little thirsty from all these cheers for our team."

Marjorie is indeed thirsty so she knows this is no lie. Smoothing her petticoats so that she remains 'ladylike' as she stands up Marjorie adds, "I am going to go to the concession stand to get a drink."

Always the thoughtful one Marjorie offers, "Would you like a drink too, Mary?"

Mary tears her eyes away from the game long enough to respond, "Do you want me to come with you, Marj?"

Rolling her eyes backwards, Marjorie frowns at her friend and reminds her, "It is Marjorie, silly girl. You know I hate the names Marj, or Marjie."

Mary was so intent on watching the game; her memory had failed her for the moment.

To show Mary she forgave her, Marjorie smiled and patted Mary's forehead. Then she turned Mary's head back in the direction of the team who was fighting it out on the ten-yard line. Smiling at the back of her head Marjorie does her friend a favor by adding, "That's okay, Mary. I can go by myself."

Marjorie's friend was pretty, too. Marjorie did not want to take any chances with this handsome man. Therefore, with all the grace she could muster, what with these darn hard bleachers and all, Marjorie skips off to the concession stand.

Marjorie says a little prayer to God that the handsome man who has her all mushy inside will wait for her. If only she knew. As she is making her way through the crowded stadium, Marjorie tries to calm herself. Her heart is beating so fast at the thought of taking such an unusual step because Marjorie is not usually this, 'bold kind of a person.'

'Be still my heart,' Marjorie tells herself, 'you can do this.' With one hand twirling her hair, she walks quickly to the Concession stand.

Taking her place in line as she reaches her destination, Marjorie stands on her tiptoes to read the signs that display the items that are for sale. Marjorie wears glasses but sometimes she still has to focus hard to read that far away.

Marjorie is so intent on reading the menu that at first, she does not hear the footsteps, nor did she notice the person who creeps around her with a smile and steals her place in line. With his hands on his hips, Kilmer Jr. adjusts his jacket and pretends to study the same menu as Marjorie.

Taking a step backwards, Kilmer Jr. bumps into this beautiful girl. With a shy smile, Kilmer grins at Marjorie and then turns his attention back to his order.

Marjorie's palms begin to twitch with excitement and she feels her heart leap into her throat. 'How can I meet him?' Marjorie asks herself. 'What can I do to make him turn around again?'

Then with a toss of her head, she gathers her thoughts and finds the answer. Marjorie Jane Powers knew that if she sneezes a gentleman would offer his handkerchief.

So as dainty as it is brave, Marjorie sneezes with a flourish, "Achoo."

Kilmer Oscar Moe Jr. was about to prove that he is indeed, a gentleman. With a twinkle in his eyes and his hand in his pocket, Kilmer Jr. pulls out his handkerchief; grateful that is was still clean and perfectly pressed.

Kilmer Jr. offers Marjorie the solution to her sneeze and says, "Oh, bless you, would you like my handkerchief?"

Marjorie sniffs and says with a smile, "Yes, please."

As she accepts the handkerchief from this handsome stranger, their fingers touch. Feeling flustered, Marjorie pretends to blow her nose. Peering through her fingers at Kilmer Jr. Marjorie could see that their touch had meant something to him as well.

Introducing herself Marjorie Jane smiles and politely holds out her hand, "Hello, my name is Marjorie Jane Powers."

Because he had finally overcome the lump in his throat, Kilmer Jr. responds by saying, "Hello. My name is Kilmer Moe, but everybody calls me Kim. Are you enjoying the game?"

Marjorie is an honest girl. She always tries to capture what is in her heart by speaking carefully but directly. Marjorie answers his question as she chews on the end of her ponytail, "No, I just came to the football game because my roommate wanted to."

Kilmer Jr. did not care why she came. At that moment, all he cared about was the fact that Marjorie had walked into his life. With gratitude Kilmer Jr. replies, "Well, would you like to go somewhere for a soda?"

Marjorie cocks her head to one side as was her habit and shyly stammers, "I would love to but I cannot leave my friend here all by herself."

Feeling relieved that she had not turned him down Kilmer Jr. tries to be helpful and replies, "Well, I have a friend. Maybe we could take the friend out with the friend."

Smiling Marjorie had to mouth the words, "Okay," because there was sudden roar coming from the crowd as the home team scored a touchdown. Marjorie Jane Powers slips her hand into Kilmer Oscar Moe's offered arm and turns with him to walk towards their bleachers. Finding their friends and collecting their belongings, Marjorie, and Kilmer Jr. journey on to a future that begins with this one fateful night.

Kilmer Jr. and Marjorie make a handsome couple and they went everywhere together. She was not only his soul mate; Marjorie was also Kilmer Jr.'s self-proclaimed best friend. Since the night they met, Kilmer Jr. had not had eyes for another and Marjorie in return.

Kilmer Jr. and Marjorie skip across campus together, barefoot. Kilmer Jr. hated to wear shoes. Growing up in Hawaii, everyone in the Islands went barefoot. Marjorie would giggle when she would see Kilmer Jr. immediately remove his shoes after class. Pointing to her feet Kilmer Jr. would smile at Marjorie and together they would sit down under the cool, campus shade trees. There Kilmer Jr. would take off Marjorie's shoes. In return, Marjorie would make Kilmer Jr. laugh by tickling his feet.

Pulling Marjorie to her feet, Kilmer Jr. would smile proudly at her as she walked barefoot next to him. Enjoying the cool grass under their feet, they would head to the library.

Marjorie and Kilmer Jr. studied as they held hands and talked of their mutual desires for a career in teaching. Kilmer Jr. wanted to teach Shop and Marjorie had her heart set on teaching Home Economics.

Kilmer Jr. asked her, "Why do you love Home Economics, Marjorie?"

Marjorie responded with words that made his mouth water, "Because I can bake with the best of 'em and if you ever taste one of my cakes, you will be in love with me forever."

Kilmer Jr. had to laugh at that one. Marjorie Jane Powers had already won his heart for so many other reasons she did not even know about. One thing was for sure; Kilmer Jr. knew he would never forget the first time Marjorie made dinner for him.

They had been dating for six months when Marjorie prepared a meal of a tender, rare roast beef surrounded by baby red tomatoes and potatoes. She then topped the meat off with homemade gravy swirled with baked onions. Kilmer Jr. knew Marjorie was his destiny all right.

With a grin, Kilmer Jr. remembered the cake Marjorie had served with a flourish. After asking Kilmer Jr. which cake was his favorite, Marjorie surprised him at that first dinner by making him one. Kilmer Jr. loved Angel Food cake but his choice that night was a Black Forest cake. Kilmer Jr. knew it was a difficult cake to make so he was not expecting much. To his amazement, that cake was the lightest, most delicious cake; he 'ever had the pleasure of dipping his fork into.' Marjorie was indeed right about her skills in the kitchen.

Kilmer Jr. held Marjorie's hand and told his girl with a grin, "Honey, if I wasn't in love with you before, I surely am in love with you now." Kilmer Jr. was teasing her, of course. He loved everything about his Marjorie.

Kilmer Jr.'s eyes were intense as he shared with Marjorie how much he loved the way she would hang on his every word when he talked about this or that. Kilmer Jr. is not a tall man but his girl made him feel six feet tall the way she watched him as he spoke. Why, that girl would look at him as if he were the only man in the world, no matter how crowded the room might be. Kilmer Jr. walked a little taller, and held his girl's hand a little tighter, just knowing Marjorie was his.

After that date from their first homemade dinner, Kilmer Jr. said good night to his Marjorie with a tender good night kiss, the first of many to come. Kilmer Jr. held Marjorie's hands, swinging them back and forth; as he told her, he loved everything about her.

Tenderly and with regret, Kilmer Jr. left Marjorie at her dorm. With a full heart, he walked back to his car. Kilmer Jr. knew that this beautiful Angel would hold his heart for all eternity. With excitement, Kilmer Jr. found himself whistling as he began to plan their future together.

Marjorie heard that whistle and leaned out the window to watch Kilmer Jr. walk away. Marjorie just loved the way her guy walked with such a spring in his step and his head held high.

Marjorie's heart was full from the words of love that Kilmer Jr. had just a whispered in her ear. She found herself thinking, 'I am falling in love with him as well.'

Marjorie turned and leaned against the ledge that held the window. She smiled to herself and thought, 'Kilmer Jr. has taught me so much about life. He knows so much about all the animals we see when we go for a walk on the trails.'

Marjorie pulled her sweater around her shoulders against the cool breeze coming down the hall. She loved the way her Kilmer Jr. was so romantic! He would bring her flowers all the time and more often than not, Kilmer Jr. picked them himself.

Kilmer Jr. knew the names of all the beautiful treasures in his bouquet. He would point to each one and share its history and beauty with Marjorie. Marjorie would gaze into his eyes and listen intently to the man who was stealing her heart.

Marjorie learned that Kilmer Jr. was born in the Philippines but he grew up in Hawaii. One day, Kilmer Jr. had an Orchid flown in from his native land. He presented this Orchid to the love of his life. As Marjorie accepted this delicate flower, she realized how difficult it must have been for Kilmer Jr. to arrange her surprise. To Kilmer Jr.'s amazement, Marjorie fell for this beautiful gift of nature and the Orchid would remain her favorite flower for the rest of her life.

Walking to her room, Marjorie thought about the way Kilmer Jr. could whistle. Marjorie had tried and tried to master the technique but failed. Unlocking her door Marjorie thought to herself, 'I wonder if Kilmer Jr. can teach me to whistle as he can.' With a grin, Marjorie said good night to her roommate, Mary, and tucked herself into bed. Rolling over Marjorie welcomed the dreams she knew would be of her guy and their future together.

Driving home that night, Kilmer Jr. thought about all the little things he loved about his Marjorie. She was every inch a lady. Kilmer Jr. loved the way she would chew on her hair and her nails when she was nervous. It was just so cute the way Marjorie would twirl her hair around and around her little finger, then pop in it between her lips for a good chew. Kilmer Jr. would wrinkle his nose at Marjorie, and with a smile and a tender gesture; remove said curl from her mouth. Marjorie would give her guy a quick wink and try her best to stop 'a-twirlin.'

Before she knew it though, Marjorie would move on to smacking her nails between her lips. Sneaking a peek at Kilmer Jr. to see if he noticed, Marjorie would grin if he caught her. What Kilmer Jr. did not know about his girl was that she chewed her nails on purpose. Marjorie loved the way Kilmer Jr. would remove the offending hand out of her mouth, hold out each little finger, and dropped a kiss onto the end of it. After each finger had received his loving, Kilmer Jr. would wrap his hand around hers and deliver it into his pocket; for safekeeping, Kilmer Jr. thought. To make her heart pound, Marjorie knew.

One year after they met, Marjorie knew it was time to take Kilmer Jr. home to meet her mom and dad. Marjorie called her mother, Mildred Powers, with an announcement that brought Marjorie mixed feelings. Marjorie is excited at the prospect of introducing Kilmer Jr. to her family. Troubling Marjorie, however, is the agreement she made with her dad in which she was not to have a steady boyfriend until after she graduates from college.

Robert Powers wants only the best for his girls and he knows that one of the answers is for Marjorie and Rosemary to get a degree before they settle down. Marjorie is nervous about her dad's reaction but she makes that call to her mother.

Mildred assures her daughter that everything will be okay once Robert sees the wonderful way that Kilmer Jr. treats their daughter. To Marjorie's surprise, Mildred and Robert Powers invite them both over for a weekend visit.

Finally, the big day arrives. Kilmer Jr. bundles Marjorie into his car for this ride into his future. Smiling to himself, Kilmer Jr. pats the ring in his pocket to make sure it is still there. Kilmer Jr. has wanted to ask Marjorie to marry him for quite some time now. He knows she is the only girl he will ever love and everything he wants out of life.

Marjorie is a lady--his lady and he has always treated her as such. Kilmer Jr. is a gentleman. Kilmer Jr. knows the right thing to do is to ask Marjorie's Dad for his permission first. If Marjorie's Dad gives him his blessings, Kilmer Jr. knew he could then respectfully ask Marjorie to be his bride.

Kilmer Jr. begins to smile but covers his mouth with his hand. He does not want Marjorie to guess something is up; Kilmer Jr. wants to surprise his girl when he gets down on one knee. Kilmer Jr. can barely keep his secret to himself because since their first date, Kilmer Jr. has always shared his thoughts, hopes, and dreams with Marjorie. This little black box holds not just the ring inside but also his heart that goes with it. Chewing on his lip to keep it from curling, Kilmer Jr.

puts his arm around his girl and they begin the long journey to Marjorie's hometown.

On the drive to meet Marjorie's parents, Kilmer Jr. decided he had to win over Marjorie's family. Once he has Robert's blessings, Kilmer Jr. knows in his heart that Marjorie would like a proposal to come about in Robert and Mildred's home. On this trip, therefore, Kilmer Jr. wants to ask his Marjorie to become Mrs. Kilmer Oscar Moe Jr.

A tear springing to his eyes, Kilmer Jr. imagines the way his moment would unfold. Marjorie is standing before him as he gets down on one knee. When he opens the little black box, Kilmer Jr. knew Marjorie would begin to cry. Kilmer Jr. also knows Marjorie would say, 'Yes,' when he asks Marjorie Jane Powers, the only woman he will ever love, to marry him.

VISION 6 SHE SNEEZES

The following story is a vision describing the beginning of the romance between Richard's Mom, Marjorie Jane Powers Moe, and Richard's Dad, Kilmer Oscar Moe Jr., whom I refer to as 'Dad' or 'Daddy'. Marjorie Jane Powers Moe, I refer to as 'Mom.' The 'Robert' I refer to is Marjorie's Dad, Robert Irvin Powers, and Richard's maternal Grandfather. The 'Mildred' I refer to is Marjorie's Mom and Richard's maternal Grandmother, Mildred Rupert Powers.

Jane: Mom was at the stands at the...What was it? It was a football game where they were going to school.

Richard: I understand.

Jane: Mom was with her very best friend and Kilmer Oscar Moe Jr.; (Daddy) said she had on this skirt. It has called a poodle skirt. It has a...the little...huh? It had Petticoats under it. Mom had on white bobby socks, she had on white shoes, and the Poodle on the skirt was white. Mom was also wearing a white and red blouse. Dad says that Mom looked beautiful with a long ponytail.

Mom was sitting there and she was talking to her friend at the game. Your dad went by with his buddies. Dad looked up and he saw Mom. Dad thought Mom was the most beautiful little angel he has ever seen.

Richard: I see.

Jane: Mommy said that she could feel somebody staring at her. She looked down and she saw a handsome man. She remembered him from the donut shop. Dad had these big ears sticking out and Mom fell in love with him right away.

Richard: How cute is that?

Jane: I am asking them, well how did you two start talking? I am trying to listen to them but they are both talking at once.

Richard: Isn't it ladies first?

Jane: You would think.

Richard chuckles.

Jane: What a cute story, Mom. The Mommy was watching to see where Dad was going to sit. She saw that he was sitting with a whole bunch of guys and she was a little bit too...Mom was a little bit shy to go around all those guys, so she's thinking, 'How can I meet him?' Mom was watching Dad and she saw him leave the group.

Mom saw Dad going to the delicatessen stand so Mom said to her friend, Mary, 'May I have a nickel, please, because I'm really thirsty?'

Her friend gives her a nickel and then she says, 'Do you want me to go with you to get the drink?'

Mom says, 'No, thank you.'' Mom did not tell her why she was going because her friend was pretty, too.

Mom did not want her friend to get the handsome man. Mom said, 'No, thank you,' like that.

Mom takes the nickel, she is so...kind of scared and her legs were trembling because she is doing this bold thing. Mom is not really a bold kind of a person but she wanted to meet Dad so she goes up there. Mom has her nickel and she is standing in line. Dad is right in front of her, Mom does not know what to do, and so she sneezes, 'Achoo,' like that.

Mom says back then the boys would hand you their handkerchief and boy he did. Dad turned right around and he saw it was the beautiful woman....Dad's calling her a girl right now...most beautiful girl he's ever seen and Dad says, 'Oh, bless you, would like my handkerchief?'

Mom goes, 'Oh, thank you so much.'

Dad handed Mom the handkerchief and then he said, 'Are you enjoying the game?'

Mom said, 'No, I just came to the game because my friend likes to.'

Huh? I know that part, Dad. Then the handsome man said, 'Would you like to go for a soda?'

Mom says, 'Yes, I would because I don't like the game but I can't leave my friend here all by herself.'

The Daddy says, 'Well, I have a friend. Maybe we could bring the friend?'

Okay, okay, I understand. 'Maybe we could bring the friend with the friend.' The friends all go out together and they had a great time that night.

Richard: Good.

Jane: I told him that part, Dad. The Mommy wants me to tell you that Daddy had on this cute shirt. Mom will never forget how handsome he looked. Dad had on a jacket with the letter on it. It was a brown jacket and it had letters on it for the school. It was a little bit chilly out that night and Dad took his jacket off and put it around Mom's shoulders because she was cold.

Richard: I see.

Jane: Yes, that is what they remember.

Richard: How sweet is that? That is a beautiful story.

Jane: Mom and Dad both had on the same brand of socks. They wore matching bobby socks. Mom and Dad noticed it that night and they decided that was a sign.

Richard: How sweet is that?

Jane: I like that story.

Richard: That is a nice story.

Jane: Mom and Dad like that story, too. They were both talking at once.

Richard: I see that.

Jane: It gets so hard to follow.

Richard: You did a good job, Honey.

Jane: Did you like that story, Son?

Richard: I loved that story, Mom and Dad.

Jane: He loves that story. Yeah. Now I can have another cookie.

Both Richard and Jane are chuckling.

Richard: Don't tell Dad.

Jane: He is right here.

Richard: I see.

Jane: He says that I deserve one because I am being patient, which is not easy.

Richard: Richard laughs and the tape turns off.

VISION 7 DID YOU KISS HIM?

In the following vision, I am asking Richard's Mom, Marjorie Jane Powers Moe, whom I refer to as 'Mom,' about the first time she met Richard's Dad, Kilmer Oscar Moe Jr., whom I refer to as 'he' and 'his.'

Richard: What are you asking Mom?

Jane: Did she kiss Dad good night?

Richard: I see.

Jane: Mom says no, but Dad held her hand.

Richard: I understand.

Both Jane and Richard chuckle.

Jane: How sweet is that?

Richard: That is sweet.

Jane: Mom felt warm and snuggly when she wore Dad's coat because it smelled like him.

Richard: I see.

Jane: That's so cute, Mom.

Richard: That is such a sweet story.

VISION 8 I LIKE THIS BOY

This vision is the story in which Marjorie Jane Powers Moe, Richard's Mom, whom I refer to as 'Mommy' or 'Mom,' takes her then boyfriend, Kilmer Oscar Moe Jr., Richard's Dad, whom I refer to as 'Dad' or 'the Dad,' home to meet Marjorie's parents the first time. The 'Robert' I refer to is Marjorie's Dad and Richard's maternal Grandfather, Robert Irvin Powers. 'The Mildred' I refer to is Marjorie's Mom and Richard's maternal Grandmother, Mildred Rupert Powers. This vision is a continuation of the 'Most Beautiful Angel' story.

Jane: Do you remember the story when the Dad and the Mom meet? I left off at the part where your dad goes to Mommy's house to meet her parents, and to give Mom the engagement ring. They told you part of the story. They want to tell you the rest of it.

Richard: Yes, I remember. You were too tired and I did not get the whole story.

Jane: That is what they said. The Mommy, she was in school. They went home to meet Mom's parents.

The Mommy says she was more scared than the Daddy was. The Mommy was a little bit nervous and a little bit scared because she was not supposed to have a boyfriend, yet. This boyfriend; she was taking your Dad home to meet her daddy and her mommy and she was scared.

Your daddy says he was not scared because he knows inside that he is a good person and he knows how much he loves your mommy. Dad believes that it is right and Mom is his soul mate. Dad knew that from the very beginning.

That is so wonderful, Dad, that is beautiful.

Dad says, yes, you do not have to be scared when the truth is there. The truth will set you free. Never be afraid.

Richard: Yes.

Jane: That is a good lesson, Daddy. Your mom and dad went into the house for a while and then the Daddy went out to the car to get the suitcases.

Your daddy says to the Robert, 'I will sleep in the car because I don't think I should sleep in the same house as your daughter. I have a lot of respect for her.' The Daddy starts to walk away.

The Robert's eyes get a little bit wet. He turns to the Mildred and he says to the Mildred, 'It will be okay. I like this boy.'

Robert walks up to the Daddy. He does not call him 'the Daddy.' What do you call him? That is so cute! Robert says, 'Come back here, Son. Come back here. We welcome you under our roof.'

Your mommy, who has red eyes too, goes running back, and says to her Honey, 'They welcome you under their roof.'

Then Mom, Dad, Mildred, and Robert all went inside and they are so happy to be together. They lit the fire in the fireplace because it was a little bit chilly out. The fire is real in the fireplace. They got out the little pillows for the ladies. The guys, they sit on the sofa next to them, and they roast marshmallows.

Robert and Mildred's little doggie jumps up and says, 'I want some. I want some.' The doggie has these long ears and the Mildred says, 'Watch out. Get away from the fire, there.'

'Lady,' that is the doggie's name, sits down. She does not want to get her ears burnt. Then the Mommy and the Mildred each give the doggie a marshmallow. It was a lovely night.

The girls walk to Marjorie's bedroom. Mildred goes in with the Mommy and says, 'Okay, girl talk time.' They were the best of friends. They had girl talk all the time and told stories. The Mommy had already told the Mildred that she had a boyfriend but they did not tell the Robert. They were scared about telling Robert.

The Robert calls to the Mildred and the Mildred says, 'I am coming, Dear.' She turns to the Mommy and says, 'Wait right here.' Mildred already knows what your dad is going to say. The Daddy had already told the Mildred what he was going to say to the Robert.

Mildred says to your mommy, 'Stay right here. I'll be right back.'

Your mommy starts to come too, but the Mildred says, 'No. Stay right here.'

Your mommy thinks, 'What is going on? What's up with that?'

Jane: (crying) that is so cute. The Mildred is telling me this. I need to tell the story but I cannot listen to four at once.

Richard: I know. Just take your time.

Jane: They are making me cry.

Jane: The Mildred comes back to the sofa. She has a big smile on her face and the Robert says to her, 'What are you grinning about?' He says it just like that.

The Mildred says, 'We're just having the girl talk in the other room and I'm just a-smiling from that.'

The Robert turns to your dad and says, 'Son, you wanted to ask us something?'

Jane: (crying again) The Son says...the Son is not really his son. Robert calls Dad Son, like that, because he welcomes him in the house.

Robert says what? I know that part, Dad. I can tell that part without crying.

Jane: (crying again) Dad says to the Robert, 'I ask you for your son...'Okay, Dad tell me one more time.

Jane: The Daddy says to the Robert, 'I want to ask for your daughter's hand in marriage.'

Richard: I see.

Jane: He really is a little bit scared right then. The Daddy, he does not know what the Robert is going to say.

The Robert says to him, 'Do you love my daughter?' Okay, the Robert says in a deep voice, 'You love my daughter?'

The Mildred says, 'I want to know that, too. Do you love my daughter?'

The Robert says, 'Tell the truth, Son.'

Your daddy says, 'I love her with all my heart because she is my soul mate.'

WHAT HEAVEN IS LIKE

Jane: (crying harder) The Son stands up and says, 'May I?'

The Robert says, 'I love her too, but she's not my soul mate and it's time for me to let her go.'

The Mildred, she is so happy. She jumps up and hugs the Son and she hugs the Robert. Mildred goes running back to the, okay, okay, she starts to go running back to the bedroom.

The Robert grabs her by the wrist and says, 'No, Mildred, it is not for you to tell.'

The Mildred goes, 'Okay, I'm sorry, I just got so excited.'

The Robert says to the Son, 'Do you have a ring, Son?'

The Son pulls out the ring and says, 'Yes, Sir, I do.'

The Robert says, 'Please, go in there and ask her. You have my blessing.'

Please, Dad. I want to tell that part now. (Sigh) They have to save the rest for another time, the part where the Daddy asks the Mommy because it is a long part.

Richard: I understand. Thank you, Mom and Dad.

Jane: They are making my nose run now.

Richard: Thank you, Grandpa, and Grandma.

Jane: What do you mean? That is not the Grandma and the Grandpa talking. That is the Mildred and the Robert.

Richard: That is my Grandma and Grandpa.

Jane: No, you are not even born, yet.

Richard: I know. Okay, then they are not the Grandma and Grandpa. They are the Robert and the Mildred.

Richard: I understand. I am born now.

Jane: They say, 'Do you like that story, Son?'

Richard: I love that story!

Jane: That story made me cry. They are making my nose run and that made me very happy. That is a lovely story.

Richard: I love those kinds of stories, Mom and Dad. I love those stories very much.

Marjorie Jane Powers   **Kilmer Oscar Moe Jr.**

VISION 9 WILL YOU MARRY ME?

This vision is the story in which Kilmer Oscar Moe Jr., Richard's Dad, whom I refer to as 'Dad' or 'the Dad,' proposes to Richard's Mother, Marjorie Jane Powers Moe, whom I refer to as 'Mommy' or 'Mom' at the home of Marjorie's parents. The 'Robert' I refer to is Marjorie's Dad and Richard's maternal Grandfather, Robert Irvin Powers. 'The Mildred' I refer to is Marjorie's Mom and Richard's maternal Grandmother, Mildred Rupert Powers.

121

Jane: Here is a story about the big engagement time.

Richard: I see.

Jane: The Mommy was in the bedroom. Robert asked the Daddy if he has a ring to give to the Mommy.

Jane: The Daddy says, 'Yes, Sir, I do.'

Robert says, 'Go in there and ask her.'

The Daddy went to the bedroom. He knocked on the door and the Mommy thinks it is her mommy. She opens the door. She is a little shy because the Daddy has never come into her bedroom before.

She says, 'I can't let you come in here because it is my bedroom.'

The Daddy says, 'I know. I have Robert's blessing.'

Mommy says, 'Do you have blessings to come in the bedroom?'

The Daddy laughs and says, 'Not like you think. He gave me permission to come in and talk to you for a minute.'

Your mom is getting very confused because she does not know what is going on. What is he going to say? 'I am so confused,' she says to herself.

She looks down the hall at her mom. Her mom is closing the door. Her mom has this big beaming face and she winks at her. All of a sudden, the Mommy starts getting little butterflies.

She starts to think, 'Oh my goodness, this is something monumental in my lifetime. Something special is coming right now. What could it be? What could it be? Maybe he's going to break up with me or maybe he will say he wants to move away.' Maybe, maybe, just maybe in the back of her mind, could it be?

Your mom is getting so dizzy with excitement that she starts making little tiny...I forgot that word, chitchat, she makes little tiny chitchats because she does not know what to say.

The Daddy comes up to her, takes both of her hands, and very sweetly says, 'Sit down, my love. Here, sit down in your childhood rocker.'

The Mommy sits down. He is very mature right now, very strong, very handsome, and very much in control. She likes it and she is very attracted to him right now.

I can say that, Dad. He is just turning her on. Dad, it is okay if I say that. It is a nice romantic part and in a little bit of a funny way. It is somewhat nice. I like that.

The Mommy says to herself, 'This might be the night.' She does not have to wait very long.

Her Honey comes up to her and takes her face into his hands and he looks down at the Mommy.... (Jane: crying) I know, Dad.

He says, 'The first time I saw you; I thought you were the most beautiful little Angel. I loved you from the moment I saw you and I knew I wanted to make you my very own.'

Mom is not saying anything because she knows this is his moment and she is listening.

He said, 'I asked your dad for your hand in marriage tonight and he gave me his blessing.'

The Mommy is so excited. She has little worms inside her stomach and butterflies jumping up and down. She is waiting and waiting, breathlessly. She does not want to forget this moment the rest of her life.

He says, 'I know I can't give you the whole world and I know that we won't be wealthy. I will not be able to buy you a large mansion like the ones the movie stars have. If the amount of love I have means anything at all, I can buy you the moon, the skies, and the heaven.'

The Mommy starts crying and says, 'That's all I want out of life, is that and you.'

He takes the ring out of his jacket and holds it towards her. He gets down on one knee, 'Will you marry me, Marjorie Jane Powers?'

She looks at the ring and then she looks at him and says, 'I would love you and I would marry you even if there wasn't such a beautiful ring.' Then they both start laughing because of the silly moment. He pulls her up, gets off his knees, and says, 'I'll always love you.'

Then they hug and kiss, and hug and kiss, and they hug and kiss, and hug and kiss, and hug and kiss. I can say that part. These are the most sensuous kisses that they had up to this moment. Your mom says her knees were weak, her arms were shaking, and she felt your dad's manhood for the first time. I am not supposed to tell you that part. She says that was a very different moment in their life. She did not know what that felt like before. She says from that moment on she would always be the luckiest woman for the rest of her life.

Richard: How sweet is that?

Jane: Everybody is crying and the Robert is saying, 'I didn't know about that part.' He talks in a deep voice like that. 'I didn't know about that part.'

The Mom says, 'Well?'

The Mildred says, 'She had to know about it sometime. Otherwise, on their honeymoon it's going to be a surprise.'

Robert says, 'I hope that wasn't too big of a surprise,' and that lightens the moment again.

Everything was wonderful. She said that Robert and Mildred brought out a little engagement cake. They sat around and ate the cake.

The Robert said to the Mildred, 'You knew about this all the time, Mildred.'

Mildred, 'No, I just got this cake for no reason at all.'

The Robert said, 'You did?'

Mildred, 'I'm teasing you, Robert.'

Robert, 'I see. Why did you keep this secret from me, Mildred?'

Mildred says, 'The reason is because it was a girl secret and we didn't want to spoil the moment for you.'

Richard: Wow, this is a special story.

Jane: The next day the girls went looking for the wedding dress and bridesmaid dresses. The boys stayed home, watched football games, and smoked stogies. They do not like stogies but they smoked them anyway. They had to go outdoors.

Richard: That is a special story.

Jane: It is a beautiful story.

Richard: Thank you, Mom, and Dad.

Jane: I left out one part. Mom says I should tell you this was the most romantic moment of her life.

Richard: How sweet is that?

Jane: She cherishes those moments and she looked at the ring and said it was the most beautiful ring that she has seen. She told her Honey if she had to pick out a ring, the ring he got her is exactly the one that she would have picked out. He was so proud because he picked it out by himself.

Richard: That is a big decision.

Jane: It was a very big decision, he says. In addition, he says that he was glad he went by himself even though his dad, Grandpa Moe, wanted to go with him. He wanted to do it all on his own because this woman--he was getting all on his own.

Richard: That is such a special story.

Jane: That is a very special story.

Richard: Thank you. I love that story. That is a beautiful story. It is so nice to know these stories. Is it time for you to rest?

Marjorie Jane Powers & Kilmer Oscar Moe Jr.

VISION 10 DAD HAD MOM IN HIS EYES

This vision is the story in which Kilmer Oscar Moe Jr., Richard's Dad, whom I refer to as 'Dad' or 'the Dad,' gets married to Richard's Mother, Marjorie Jane Powers Moe, whom I refer to as 'Mommy,' 'her,' 'she,' or 'Mom.' The reference to 'Mom's Dad' is to Marjorie's Father and Richard's maternal Grandfather, Robert Irvine Powers. The reference I make to 'her mom' is Marjorie's Mother and Richard's maternal Grandmother, Mildred Rupert Powers.

127

Jane: They are going to take us back to where they got married.

Richard: Good. I want to hear about that.

Jane: Yes. Her favorite color for her bridesmaids was pink and maroon. Those were the colors for the wedding.

Richard: So, her bridesmaids wore pink.

Jane: They wore, what's the other one. They wore maroon and pink.

Richard: Wow, that's beautiful.

Jane: Yes, it is beautiful.

Richard: I understand.

Jane: Those are her favorite colors. She wishes she hadn't chosen such an ugly dress for her bridesmaids but they looked just fine in them.

Richard: Good.

Jane: Yes, she had two of them, two girls.

Richard: She had two girls?

Jane: Yes, she had two girls: Wendy and Mary.

Richard: The girl's names were Wendy and Mary.

Jane: She had to practice to go down the aisle, to go slow, because you are supposed to go: step one, step one.

Richard: I understand.

Jane: Step one, step one, and she practiced with her daddy, but she did not want to go slow. She wanted to go running right up there and marry your dad.

Richard: I see.

Jane: She was so happy. It was a beautiful day and the Sun was shining. She woke up that morning and she said, 'Today, I'm going to be Mrs. Moe.'

Richard: How cute is that?

Jane: She was so happy but a little bit nervous. She did not know what she was getting into. Her Mommy did not want to tell Mom 'cause back then; everything was kept a secret.

Richard: I see.

Jane: She was a little scared.

Richard chuckles

Jane: She said that she had the most beautiful white dress that you ever saw and that it had the bells around the bottom. They are not really bells; it is what they called the lace.

Richard: I see.

Jane: No, it is just a name.

Richard: I see.

Jane: It means that they hang down in lacy pieces and that she had an umpire, empire, what is the difference. It was an empire waistline dress.

Richard: Wow!

Jane: She had a fingertip length for the top. It was a beautiful dress. Her mom gave her the something old and something new.

Richard: I see.

Jane: Mom's Dad gave her something borrowed and something blue.

Richard: I see.

Jane: That's so cute, Mom. The Daddy wore a beautiful maroon suit.

Richard: I understand.

Jane: Daddy looked handsome in the suit but he was so uncomfortable.

Richard chuckles.

Jane: He kept pulling on his neck and he kept saying, 'My feet are killing me.' He was wearing the shoes that came with the suit. He hates wearing shoes.

Richard: Yes, that's my dad.

Jane: He had on brown socks. He was sweating because his feet are not used to wearing socks. He was sweating so much that his toes turned brown from the socks.

Richard chuckles.

Jane: He was nervous, too.

Richard: Yes.

Jane: The Daddy has short hair and he got it cut even shorter for the wedding.

Richard: I see.

Jane: The Mommy has her ponytail.

Richard: Is that right?

Jane: She brushed her ponytail until it was shinny. She put on Alberto VO 5. They had that back then and it made her hair shiny.

Richard: Wow.

Jane: What is Alberto, Alberto VO 5? It makes your hair shiny.

Richard: Wow.

Jane: I do not know what that is. I see, like baby oil. She says, do you remember that?

Richard: Alberto VO 5?

Jane: She put it in your hair to make your cowlick stay in place.

Richard chuckles

Jane: It never did.

Richard: Wow.

Jane: It still does not.

Richard: She used to wet her fingers and put it on my hair.

Jane: She is telling me that right now and that you hated that.

Richard chuckles

Jane: You would be the 'little tyke' trying to run away.

Richard: I see.

Jane: She could never make your hair behave, anyway.

Richard: I know.

Jane: He does not behave now either, Mom.

Richard chuckles.

Jane: She says she knows. Her favorite dance of her whole lifetime was the first dance that she danced with your dad when she was Mrs. Moe.

Richard: How sweet is that?

Jane: She had stars in her eyes.

Richard: I understand.

Jane: Dad said he had Mom in his eyes.

Richard: How sweet is that?

Jane: Tell me about that night, Mom.

Jane and Richard laugh.

Jane: She is getting red in the face. Did you get the Bob that night?

Richard: Yes?

Jane: They went out to the cars. Somebody had tied old shoes on the car.

Richard: Really?

Jane: When they drove the car away, the shoes went thump, thump, and thump.

Richard: I see.

Jane: They had confetti on the car and balloons tied on the antenna.

Richard: Wow.

Jane: Somebody wrote, 'Just married,' on the balloons.

Richard: I see, how cute!

Jane: The balloons on the car were pink and maroon.

Richard: The balloons were the same color as the girl's dresses.

Jane: That was her, what do you call it?

Richard: Theme?

Jane: Yes, it was her theme. She says it was her theme from the wedding.

Richard: Yes.

Jane: Pink is for the love in her heart.

Richard: I see. Was it at the school? Where they went to college?

Jane: Where was the chapel? The chapel was in the town where they went to church.

Richard: I see.

Jane: Dad did not go to that church. It was the Mommy's church.

Richard: I understand.

Jane: Daddy came to the Mommy's church because he wanted her to be so proud of him.

Richard: I see. How sweet is that?

Jane: They got married in that church. It is a chapel. They had the rest of the wedding, the reception, at her home.

Richard: I understand.

Jane: The chapel has a steeple over the top.

Richard: What year was that?

Jane: What year was that, Mom? No, what year was the wedding? No, what year was that, Mom. She is asking your dad. Nineteen forty-eight.

Richard: The year was nineteen forty-eight?

Jane: Yes, nineteen forty-eight.

Richard: I see.

Jane: That was a long time ago.

Richard: That was before I was a twinkle in Dad's eye.

Jane: It was?

Richard: Yes.

Jane: Were you forty-eight? I see nineteen forty-eight is the year.

Richard: Yes.

Jane: I see.

Richard: Yes, I was born in nineteen fifty-three.

Jane: They had Bob twinkles right away.

Richard: They did?

Jane: Well, that is what Mommy says.

Richard: I see.

Jane: Yes. They had the Bob twinkles. They graduated from school first.

Richard: I see. Which college did they attend?

Jane: They will be right back, Honey. They are over there looking down at the baby. It is the Bob.

Richard: It is the Bob?

Jane: Yes, they are holding hands looking down at the Bob.

Richard Powers Moe
The 'Little Tyke'

CHAPTER 9 RAISING 'THE LITTLE TYKE'

Marjorie and Kilmer Moe Jr. became the proud parents of three children: Robert Kilmer Moe, born September 2, 1949, and he is married to his beautiful wife, Cheryl. Robert and Cheryl presented Marjorie and Kilmer Jr. with their only grandchildren, Jenafer Lane Moe and Robert Kacy Moe. Richard Powers Moe was born on October 6, 1953, and Kathryn Lane Moe was born May 11, 1955.

Richard Powers Moe is also my fiancé and we met at my place of employment, Arrow Tools, in Van Nuys, California. I was an outside sales person for this company who specializes in the sale of construction materials. Richard Moe was one of our customers and he would smile shyly at me and clam up.

Richard and I have a lot in common, because Richard is a wonderful concrete contractor who owns his own construction company. We would talk about the different materials he needed to build his projects and which tools I might recommend.

It took Richard a long time to ask me for a formal date. We went to Disneyland and like his mom and dad; we have been together ever since. It has been seven wonderful years. Because he was so shy at first, getting to know my handsome, sweet, and giving man has never been an easy feat.

While dating, Richard would share his feelings and emotions with me, but to get him to talk about his past or his family was like pulling teeth. I would finally learn that Richard's beloved Mother had recently passed away. When I asked Richard about his dad, it was with reluctance that Richard told me that his dad had died when he was only fifteen years old. That was all I was to learn from Richard about his dad, other than the fact that Richard's Dad had gone into a small hospital for a routine procedure and had died there from Pneumonia. After that, I could not bear to see my Richard in pain so I left the subject alone.

Getting to know Richard's parents, Marjorie and Kilmer Moe Jr., has been a wonderful experience for me. I have gotten to know them from their own eyes and I have come to love them.

Richard's first memories of his family are from his early years. Richard remembers how much he loved to be a cowboy when he was young. In my visions, I share with Richard that his mom carried a photo of him, as a little boy in his cowboy outfit, until the day she died. Richard confirms this story as I retell it in a vision. This recording I have included at the end of the chapter.

Richard did not realize that his mom had to remake this cowboy outfit three times because he kept outgrowing it. Marjorie Jane Powers Moe is a wonderful mother. She never burdened her son by telling him she had to re-make his cowboy outfit repeatedly to keep up with his growth. Quietly and lovingly, she would remake his outfit on her own sewing machine. Marjorie is quite a tailor and made her boys and her husband Pendleton-type shirts. Richard never told me this; I learned it from his mom.

Richard remembers and is thrilled as I retell his past. Having his dearly departed mom and dad back in his life again has brought Richard joy and peace.

In my visions, I retell Richard's childhood from his parent's point of view. Richard recalls these memories but in a 'childlike' sort of way. The memories are dim until I bring them back to life with the rich details.

When he was a little boy, Richard's Mom made him a Snoopy costume one year for Halloween. Richard had his heart set on being Snoopy and when they could not find the costume in the stores, Marjorie whipped it together in one evening.

In other visions, I recall for Richard his family's childhood visits to the Barnum and Bailey Circus and while there, they rode the elephants. Richard's parents love to recite their most cherished 'little tyke' stories. I become part of Richard's past as they retell their memories because I see his childhood unfold before me like an instant replay.

From his parents, I learned that Richard's Dad and he used to go fishing in Oxnard, California, on a sports fishing boat. To Richard's delight, I recall the time they caught Rock Cod. As if he did not already know it, I describe to Richard how these fish have eyes that pop out when his dad and he brought them to the surface. What I did not know until Richard explained it to me, is that these fish live deep in the water. By the time you get them up to the surface; their eyes pop out because of the change in water pressure.

Growing up, Richard and his little sister, Kathryn, were close in age and even closer as friends. When Kathryn came home from the hospital the first time, Richard's Mom explained to him that it was his job to watch over his new baby sister. Richard has always taken his responsibilities very seriously, so he watched over Kathryn and took her with him everywhere.

One night in my visions, I see Richard walking towards a store. He is pulling Kathryn behind in a little red wagon. Also in the wagon were fruits and vegetables grown at their home on Vose Street. Richard was on his way to Ralph's Grocery Store to sell his produce. The manager of this Ralph's knew a good deal when he saw one so he bought everything in the little wagon, paying Richard and Kathryn with their choice of candies.

As Richard's Mom and Dad's retelling of this story unfolds, I watch fascinated. I laugh as Kathryn eats her candy, all chocolate. Kathryn, I learned from this story, loves chocolate. Richard chose as his payment a variety of candy. He loves his red licorice but Richard saves it to eat later. Mom and Dad allowed the two to go to the grocery store but both kids could not eat their candy until after dinner. Kathryn is too young to understand she should save her candy until later. Richard, however, understands his parent's wishes. Always wanting to please his beloved mommy and daddy, Richard obediently tucked his candy away inside his little paper bag.

WHAT HEAVEN IS LIKE

Marjorie and Kilmer Jr. adore their children very much. With pride, Marjorie and Kilmer Moe Jr. share with me every accomplishment Richard has made, no matter the size. Marjorie and Kilmer Jr. have watched over their son with love and guidance since the day Richard was born. Both parents continue to do so, even after their deaths.

Richard's beloved Dad wept as he shared with us that even after his death, Kilmer Jr. is still there for his son. Kilmer Jr. once shared with me the following statement: 'Even when there is no breeze; I am the wind in Richard's hair.' Kilmer Jr. boasts of Richard's fishing skills, Richard's generosity, and Richard's kindness to everyone he meets.

Marjorie beams with joy as she sees what a gentleman her Richard has become, how he holds the door open for both men and women alike. Marjorie adds with a knowing smile, 'Richard remembers the table manners I taught him.'

Both parents are very proud of their Richard and they always will be. I can see the pride shinning in their eyes as they share their favorite 'little tyke' stories with me, retold from their hearts.

**Richard, Kilmer Jr., Robert,
Kathy, Barney, & Marjorie Moe**

VISION 11 WHAT IF HE GETS HURT?

In the following vision, Kilmer Oscar Moe Jr., Richard's
Dad, whom I refer to as 'Dad' or 'the Dad' and
Richard's Mother, Marjorie Jane Powers Moe, whom I
refer to as 'Mommy,' 'The Mom,' or 'Mom,' take their
sons, Richard Powers Moe, and his brother, Robert
Kilmer Moe, whom I refer to as 'Bob,' to the bowling

alley. Lillian, in this vision, is Richard's aunt and the only sister of Kilmer Oscar Moe Jr. I will refer to the word 'they' and I am speaking of Richard's Mom and Dad.

Jane: The Mommy says that they took you to the bowling alley so you could learn to bowl.

Richard: Yes.

Jane: You kept dropping the ball, it would go backwards, and it did not go down the alley.

Richard is laughing.

Jane: You would go running after it; you would be this 'little tyke' running, and running, and running to go after the ball. The bowling ball was bigger than you were.

Richard: Yes, I know.

Jane: You would try to throw it but you had these little hands, these little boy hands. You would try to throw it forward and it would go back behind you instead of forward. You would get so frustrated. It would go in the gutter and then finally you walked it all the way to the front where the pins are.

Richard: I see.

Jane: You threw it right where the pins are.

Richard is laughing.

Jane: The Daddy is saying, 'Son, come back here, Son. Son, come back here.'

Richard is laughing.

Jane: The Mommy is saying, 'Oh, let him be.'

The Daddy is saying, 'He's not supposed to be up there.'

The Mommy is saying, 'It's okay. Just let him be.'

The Bob is running all around saying, 'He can't be up there, he can't be up there,' like that.

Richard: I understand.

Jane: Finally, your mom said, 'Leave him be.' You got to stay up there and play around with the pins for a little while.

Richard: I remember that, I think.

Jane: Yes and the guy came down that owns the bowling alley.

Richard: I understand.

Jane: The Mommy says, 'Oh, he's not hurting anything.'

Richard is laughing

Jane: The man said, 'But what if he gets hurt?'

The Mommy says, 'Well, okay, I'll go get him.'

The Daddy says, 'No, I'll go get him.'

Richard: I see.

Jane: The Daddy goes up there to get his son. The Son starts running across all the lanes and running around another ball or two. The Mommy is saying, 'Grab him quick, before he gets hurt.'

Richard is laughing.

Jane: You were this 'little tyke' running back and forth, laughing. You thought the Daddy was trying to play, but he was not. He was trying to keep you safe.

Richard: I want to thank you for keeping me safe, Dad.

Jane is laughing.

Richard: I think I remember that. I was little. How old was I?

Jane: How old was he, Dad? You were six years old.

Richard: Six. Thank you, Daddy. Thank you, Daddy, for keeping me safe.

Jane: He says you did not want to be safe. You wanted to run around.

Richard: I know. I know.

Jane: You were running across the alleys. Moreover, the little parts with the dip in it, you started hopping over those.

Richard: I see.

Jane: The Daddy was afraid of grabbing you the wrong way because you might slip. The Mommy is saying, 'Get him, get him,' like that.

Richard is laughing.

Jane: She was so worried that the Daddy was going to fall, so she had two to worry about.

Richard: I want to thank you for that, Mom.

Richard is laughing. I love that story! I love that story.

Jane: She says, now tonight when we go bowling, you cannot do that.

Richard: No, I understand. I will be good. I will be good.

Jane: Okay, he will be good, Mom.

Richard: Yes, but I love that story. That is a good story.

Jane: The 'little tyke,' he is running around.

Richard: Yes, at six years old.

Jane: You thought the Daddy was playing a game.

Richard is laughing. I love that story. Thank you, thank you, and thank you.

Jane: I love that story, too. I got a new bowling ball.

Richard: You have a new bowling ball. That is so sweet.

Jane: The pictures of all my friends appear on it.

Richard: They sure love you.

Jane: They are my best friends.

Richard: I know they are.

Jane: Look inside the holes, it has gold in there. Lillian, did you do that? I see!

Richard: Lillian did that.

Jane: Lillian painted inside the holes with gold color.

Richard: I see. She is so special. She is so special.

**Robert Kilmer Moe
a.k.a. 'The Hurricane Tornado Child'**

VISION 12 MAKING THE GINGERBREAD

In the following vision Richard's Mother, Marjorie Jane Powers Moe, whom I refer to as 'Mommy,' 'she,' or 'Mom,' and I are making gingerbread cookies. I refer to Marjorie and me as 'we.' The 'Hurricane Tornado Child' and 'Bob' I am referring to are nicknames for Richard's brother, Robert Kilmer Moe.

Jane: We are making Gingerbread cookies.

Richard: You are. It must be almost Christmas time.

Jane: The Mommy is making the gingerbread men and the little gingerbread houses.

Richard: I see. She always made the best gingerbread houses.

Jane: That is what she is doing right now.

Richard: Really?

Jane: First, she made the gingerbread cookies. Now she is making the houses.

Richard: I loved it when she made the little houses.

Jane: I know. She is telling me how you helped.

Richard: I did help.

Jane: She is showing me how to make the little houses.

Richard: I see.

Jane: I have never watched anyone make gingerbread houses.

Richard: They are fun to make.

Jane: I like to eat them but she shoos me away. Do not eat them, yet!

Richard: No, do not eat them, yet.

Jane: They need to be finished first.

Richard: Yes.

Jane: Yes.

Richard: They have to be finished before you can eat them.

Jane: Yes.

Richard: Wow. That is a special thing. Those little houses are special.

Jane: That is what she says. You used to help her make them

Richard: Yes, I used to help her cook everything.

Jane: The 'hurricane tornado child,' Bob, would come in and pick them up. He would try to take a bite before they finished cooking.

Richard: He tried to eat them before they were finished cooking?

Jane: Yes. Mom even makes the little doors that opens and closes.

Richard: Wow!

Jane: She put the little windows in the house.

Richard: Yes, I know.

Jane: Yes, and she put in the doors.

Richard: Yeah, they were beautiful.

Jane: I know. I see it.

Richard: That was a special day.

Jane: She says, 'Do you remember doing that?'

Richard: Yes, Mom I remember doing that.

Jane: Do you remember making the houses and taking the popcorn and putting it on the string with the sewing needle?

Richard: Yes, yes, I remember the popcorn on the string.

Jane: Yes, she says, you used to do that with her.

Richard: Yes, it was beautiful.

Jane: Yes, Yes. Do not poke your fingers.

Richard: Yes. Be careful.

Jane: Yes.

Richard: Yes, I liked the popcorn on the tree. I thought that was beautiful.

Jane: She loves it, too.

Richard: Every Christmas was beautiful. Thank you, Mom.

Jane: Don't forget about the cranberries on the needle and the thread.

Richard: Yes.

Jane: That's right.

Richard: Wow that brings back happy memories, Mommy.

Jane: That is why she is telling you.

Richard: I love these stories.

Jane: The little gingerbread men, they have a little mouth.

Richard: Exactly, I remember those. They were delicious.

Jane: They have little buttons down the belly for its coat.

Richard: What did you make the buttons out of, Mom?

Jane: Red Hots.

Richard: Red Hots. Yes. Wow, those were great.

Jane: She makes the little mittens on the little gingerbread men with the little ice-pushing thing. You push up from the bottom and the little icing comes out the top.

Richard: Yes.

Jane: She could make stars with the star cap. She could make smiley faces with the smiley face cap. She could make round ones with the round one, and she could make the long streaming ones with the streaming cap.

Richard: Wow. She was very good.

Jane: Mom could bake beautifully.

Richard: I agree.

Marjorie Jane Powers Moe

VISION 13 REAL CANDLES ON THE TREE

In the following vision, I am talking about Richard's Mother, Marjorie Jane Powers Moe, whom I refer to as 'she,' and Richard's Father, Kilmer Oscar Moe Jr., whom I refer to as 'Dad.'

Jane: Do you remember the time Mom put the real lit candles on the Christmas tree?

Richard: I vaguely remember that.

Jane: She remembers. She remembers quite well.

Richard: I bet Dad remembers even better.

151

Jane: Yes, he almost got his hands burnt.

Richard: That's right.

Jane: He says that he told her, 'Whatever were you thinking?'

Richard: Well, she was excited over Christmas I think.

Jane: She says, 'Well, it'll be all right. It's just fine.'

Richard: I see.

Jane: But it was not. No, do not do that, Richard.

Richard: No, I learned from that, Mom.

Jane: That is what she says.

Richard: Thanks, Mom, for the story.

VISION 14 MOM MADE THE SHIRTS

In the following vision, I am talking about Richard's Mother, Marjorie Jane Powers Moe, whom I refer to as 'she' or 'Mom.'

Jane: She would make the most beautiful shirts.

Richard: Yes, she did.

Jane: She would put a monogram on them.

Richard: Yes.

Jane: That's right.

Richard: Yes, she made us beautiful shirts.

Jane: Yes, she made beautiful shirts with little buttons on the collars and buttons on the shirts.

Richard: Yes, they were beautiful.

Jane: Yes.

Richard: Yeah, they were beautiful. They looked like Pendleton shirts.

Jane: Yes.

Richard: I also I had my cowboy shirt.

Jane: I understand.

Richard: I loved those.

Jane: Don't forget how much you loved the cowboy hat.

Richard: Did she make the hat?

Jane: Did you make it, Mom? No, but she put the Sheriff's star on it.

Richard: I see, I see.

Jane: Yes and she put the red felt part around it. You kept wearing it so much that you kept wearing it out.

Richard: I know.

Jane: She had to keep fixing it up, sprucing it up, and you were happy with it.

Richard: Thank you, Mom. That was a great time.

Jane: 'You are welcome,' she says, 'you're welcome.' She made the little chaps for you.

Richard: I see.

Jane: So you could ride the pony.

Richard: Wow.

Jane: That is what she says.

Richard: Yeah, she did. She did.

Jane: She made the little fringe jacket.

Richard: Wow. That is special. Those were happy days, Mommy.

Jane: She says, 'Yes, they were indeed.'

Richard: I am so fortunate to have her as my mom.

Jane: She is my mom, too.

Richard: Tell her that.

Jane: You are my mom, too.

Richard: Tell her how fortunate I was to have her as my mom.

Jane: She hears you. She has the wet eyes.

Richard: Mom, you are just the best.

Marjorie Jane Powers Moe

VISION 15 HER GREENHOUSE

In the following vision, I am talking about Richard's Mother, Marjorie Jane Powers Moe, whom I refer to as 'she,' 'Mommy,' 'Marjorie,' or 'Mom.'

Jane: Do you remember helping your mommy in the garden? She says you were always out there saying, 'Can I help you, Mom? What can I do? Can I do this? Look, Mom. Look at me.'

Richard chuckles.

Jane: You would say, 'Look at me, Mom, can you see what I'm doing?' She would look to see you doing something special and then she would laugh and forget what she was doing for a minute. Then you would come rushing over and help her some more. Then you used to carry around the big old water...what do you call that. It was a pitcher of water.

Richard: I see.

Jane: It was bigger than you were. You would try to follow around behind her and carry that big old water pitcher.

Richard chuckles.

Jane: 'You knocked it over more than you helped her but she always pretended as if you were such a big help, like that. She is a good Mommy.

Richard: I liked helping her.

Jane: She remembers that the flowers in there were her favorite flowers. She had a greenhouse.

Richard: Yes, she did.

Jane: That you used to come out and say, 'Oh, so beautiful,' like that.

Richard: Yes.

Jane: What is a greenhouse, Mom? That she loved that greenhouse.

Richard: Yes, she did.

Jane: She made the most beautiful flowers right there. She raised them all by herself.

Richard: Yes, she did and on Sundays, we used to go to flower shows and buy plants.

Jane: Yes and then she would bring them home.

Richard: Yes.

Jane: And put them in her greenhouse.

Richard: Yes.

Jane: Wow.

Richard: When we moved we took that greenhouse with us.

Jane: You did. Did you, Mom? She says, 'Of course.'

Richard: Yes.

Jane: They were part of the family. That is why she made our beds out of them, out of those flowers.

Richard: I see.

Jane: It had a wooden bench out there that she liked to sit on.

Richard: That's right.

Jane: Do you remember that wooden bench? You used to climb around on it.

Richard: Yes.

Jane: She remembers. She still has that wooden bench.

Richard: Good.

Jane: Yes.

Richard: Yes, I loved the greenhouse, too.

Jane: She had her favorite flowers in there. That is when she found out, which Orchid is your favorite color. It is purplish; it is kind of a purple color.

Richard: That's right.

Jane: I know, Mom. I told him that.

Richard: All her flowers were beautiful.

Jane: She poured her love into them, she says.

Richard: Yes, she did. She did. She really cared about them.

Jane: She still has some with her.

Richard: Tell Mom when we go to see Kathryn; we take her an Orchid plant.

Jane: I understand. She knows. She sees them in the bathroom.

Richard: I see.

Jane: They get tall there because they like the water from the shower.

Richard: They last a long time.

Jane: I did not do it on purpose.

Richard: What do you mean?

Jane: She asked me why my flower died.

Richard: I see. I think our house isn't right.

Jane: It is too hot in that window. She says, 'Don't put it in the window,' like that.

Richard: I understand.

Jane: It doesn't have enough sun.

Richard: It needs more Sun.

Jane: It has too much Sun.

Richard: It has too much Sun. I see.

Jane: Don't give it so much water.

Richard: Yes.

Jane: Keep it until it gets very, very dry. Then give them a drink.

Richard: Yes. We'll try again.

Jane: Yes, Mom, we will try again.

Richard: Maybe she can help us.

Jane: She says to give it a little bit of plant food, too.

Richard: I understand.

Jane: Okay, they have a special kind of Orchid food. You get it from the store. You give them a little bit of that.

Richard: I understand.

VISION 16 REMEMBER MEXICO?

In the following vision, I am talking about Richard's Mother, Marjorie Jane Powers Moe, whom I refer to as 'she,' 'Mommy,' or 'Mom.' I am also talking about Richard's Dad, Kilmer Oscar Moe Jr., whom I refer to as 'Dad.'

Jane: Everything Mom does, she does really fast. She walks fast. She whistles fast. She races fast.

Richard: She was born fast.

Jane: Yes and when she knits something; her hands go so fast that you cannot even see them.

Richard: Yes.

Jane: I know. Here she comes.

Richard: I have a question.

Jane: I understand. Do you want me to ask her that?

Richard: Yes.

Jane: She wants to know is it for fun or is it...what did you say? Is it for fun or is it from the past?

Richard: Is it for fun or for in the past?

Jane: She says, for fun or for in the past?

Richard: Well, it's something fun and in the past.

Jane: What did you say, Mom? I understand. She says if you can ask her then could she ask you something.

Richard: Okay, all right. When we were in Mexico one time, I had some Fireworks and Cherry Bombs, and, uh, Skyrockets. Where was that? Do you remember?

Jane: Do you want me to ask her all that?

Richard: Yes.

Jane: She said you were camping.

Richard: I know, but do you know where we went camping?

Jane: Do you want me to ask her that? She says you were in Rosarita camping.

Richard: Rosarita? Wow, thanks, Mom. I was trying to remember that.

Jane: She says that she was a little bit...what? I understand. She was a little bit nervous about all the fireworks.

Richard: Yes, I had a lot of fireworks.

Jane: She told Dad that you were too little but Dad said, 'No, he's not.'

Richard: I see. Thanks, Dad.

Jane: Dad's not here. She is telling me the story.

Richard: I understand. Yes, that was a fun time.

Jane: Do you want me to tell her that?

Richard: Yes.

Jane: She says that it was a little bit scary for her but she loved that camping trip and that is what she remembers. Do you remember all the bugs that were flying in the air?

Richard: Yes.

Jane: Yes, you swatted at them. They did not hurt you. They were the kind that lit up the sky and they are your friends. Do you remember those?

Richard: Yes.

Jane: What do you call them? 'Fireflies,' she said, 'fireflies.' Yes, and you took their little butts off and you put them on your hands. You called them rings.

Richard chuckles.

Jane: Yes.

Richard: That was a fun time, Mom.

Jane repeats it to Mom, who says, 'There will be more good times to come.'

VISION 17 RIDING THE ELEPHANTS

In the following vision, I am talking about Richard's Mother, Marjorie Jane Powers Moe, whom I refer to as 'She,' 'Mommy,' or 'Mom,' and Richard's Dad, Kilmer Oscar Moe Jr., whom I refer to as 'Dad' or 'Daddy.'

Jane: She says, 'Do you remember the time you went to the circus and you rode the elephants?'

Richard: Yes, I do. Barnum and Bailey circus, is that the one?

Jane: You went to the Barnum and Bailey Circus.

Richard: Yes.

Jane: That's right.

Richard: I remember that and the elephant had a big thing on the front of his head, which said, 'Barnum and Bailey.'

Jane: It is a crown.

Richard: Okay.

Jane: Yes, that time.

Richard: Yes.

Jane: She says, "That's what I remember and that's why I likes to ride the elephants now.'

Richard: I see. I still remember that.

Jane: She remembers that, too.

Richard: That was special.

Jane: Yes.

Richard: Mom showed us many great places.

Jane: Yes.

Richard: She did this all the time.

Jane: 'Yes,' she says, 'yes.'

Richard: I remember all those places.

Jane: She liked to take you for the elephant rides and take your picture.

Richard: I see.

Jane: Her favorite picture of you is the one in which you had on a little cowboy outfit.

Richard chuckles

Jane: She carried it around and around. She still has it now.

Richard: I know. She always carried it in her wallet.

Jane: Mom always had her money just perfect, so exact.

Richard is chuckling.

Jane: Mom, you do.

Richard laughs.

Jane: Do you remember how you got the little cowboy outfit?

Richard: No, I don't.

Jane: She made it for you.

Richard: You did, Mom?

Jane: Yes, you were a cowboy one year for Halloween. You didn't want to take it off.

Richard: No?

Jane: No. That costume; Mommy made it just for you.

Richard: Yes, how special.

Jane: That costume was very, very special.

Richard: I didn't know that.

Jane: She just told me that.

Richard: I see. Now I know.

Jane: I see. She says she didn't make the gun.

Richard: No, probably not...

Jane: She did not make the boots.

Richard: She did not make the hat.

Jane: No, and she did not make the hat. She made the clothes.

Richard: I see. That was special.

Jane: Yes, it was.

Richard: I loved being a cowboy.

Jane: She says she didn't make the socks, either.

Richard laughs.

Jane: Silly Mom.

Richard: Silly Mom. Yes, I loved being a cowboy.

Jane: That's what she says.

Richard: So, that was for Halloween.

Jane: The costume was for Happy Halloween.

Jane: Do you remember that the elephant went 'poopy doop' when you were riding it? He stopped and went 'poop.'

Richard: I don't remember that.

Jane: She thought it was hilarious.

Richard: She did?

Jane: Yes.

Richard laughs.

Jane: She says to your Daddy, 'Don't step in that.'

Richard: laughing, Put your shoes on.

Jane: He didn't step in that.

Richard: I know.

Jane: He says it was the biggest 'poop' he ever saw.

Richard: I see.

Both are laughing.

Jane: Dad!

Richard: Yes, Mom, you took us to so many places: the county Arboretum where we saw the flowers, we saw plays, and we went to the beach with Dad!

Jane wakes up.

VISION 18 SOME WRONGS TO RIGHT

In the following vision, I am talking about Richard's Dad, Kilmer Oscar Moe Jr., whom I refer to as 'Dad,' 'he,' or 'him.' Also in this vision, I am talking about Richard's Mother, Marjorie Jane Powers Moe, whom I refer to as 'She,' 'Mommy,' or 'Mom.' The reference to the word 'they' is a reference to both parents.

Jane: Your dad says he is a little bit sad because you have some wrongs to right.

Richard: I have some wrongs to right?

Jane: 'Yes,' he says, 'it makes me sad.'

Richard: Which wrongs do I need to make right?

Jane: You want me to ask him that?

Richard: Yes.

Jane: He says, 'That's part of life, to learn.' We have to learn. He says, 'It's part of the circle of life.'

Richard: I understand.

Jane: The goal is to get back to our Creator. Try to live your life with honor and integrity.

Richard: I understand.

Jane: That he will always be there for you.

Richard: I know they will.

Jane: They will always be there for me, they said.

Richard: I see!

Jane: They will be there for the doggy, too.

Richard: Wow.

Jane: He's still waiting. He says, 'Barney wants to know where you are.

Richard: I will be with him someday.

Jane: I understand. Do you want me to tell him that?

Richard: Yes, and that I miss him.

Jane: I understand. (Laughing) Barney is doing the owl thing.

Richard chuckles.

Jane: So that you know, he is here.

Richard: I love that.

Jane: Now all the puppies are making that noise. It is too noisy.

Richard: How cute is that?

Jane: There are one hundred and two dogs saying that owl noise.

Richard: That's my 'Barn.'

Jane: Stop it, Barney. That is so annoying. They think it is a song.

Richard: Does Dad remember going to the Ventura Pier all the time?

Jane: Do you want me to ask him?

Richard: Yes.

Jane: I understand. Yes, he said he would take the children there on Sundays because the Mommy would have a rest.

Richard: Yes.

Jane: He said that you would go and throw rocks, you would go fishing, and that you would walk around on the pier. Those were his favorite times.

Richard: Yes, those were my favorite times, too.

Jane: That he would pick up shells and listen to them and then you would pick up the shells. You didn't know what you were listening to, but you were listening.

Richard: Yes, those were great years.

Jane: He says that to have the regrets...He has the regrets but he cannot fix them from Heaven and that he hopes that you learn from his mistakes. You cannot fix it when you leave. It is too late. I do not know what that means, Dad.

Richard: Well, all right. I will think about that. I do not understand it.

Jane: I am asking him because I do not understand it, either. He is just smiling at me saying, 'I understand. I cannot give you all the answers because you have not asked the questions.' He was feeling sadness and he had to share it with you.

Richard: I understand.

Jane: Now he is going to tuck me in.

Richard: He wants you to go to sleep.

Jane: Do you want me to tell him that? They will be here. They are not leaving yet. They are going to stay with us.

Richard: I see, and make you better?

Jane: Yes.

Richard: Good. Good.

VISION 19 USE YOUR TURN SIGNALS

In the following vision, I begin the story with 'he' and 'Dad.' I am referring to Richard's Dad, Kilmer Oscar Moe Jr. Richard's paternal Grandfather is Kilmer Oscar Moe Sr., and I refer to him as Richard's 'Grandpa Moe.' Richard's paternal Grandmother is Mable Lane Moe, and I refer to Mable as Kilmer Jr.'s 'Mommy' or 'Mom.'

Jane: He wants to know why you don't drive very safely.

Richard: I am trying to.

Jane: He is trying to, Dad. You do not use your turn signals all the time to turn the lanes and you do not keep both hands on the wheel. He is worried.

Richard: I understand. I have been working more on keeping both hands on the wheel.

Jane: He says to use your turn signals.

Richard: I understand.

Jane: He says to look over your shoulder when you change lanes.

Richard: Okay.

Jane: Because you cannot count on the...

Richard: You can't count on the mirrors.

171

Jane: 'Okay,' he said. He's worried about that. He says to tell you when you are driving you are supposed to be driving.

Richard: I understand.

Jane: Do not fidget when you are driving. You want me to tell him that. No fidgeting. He says, 'You do too many things. There is a reason that you are not supposed to use your cell phone when you are driving.'

Richard: I know.

Jane: Everyone has accidents.

Richard: Yes.

Jane: Use your turn signals.

Richard: Use my turn signals and look over my shoulder.

Jane: He says to accelerate into the turn not after the turn.

Richard: I am supposed to accelerate into the turn.

Jane: I am just telling you what he is saying.

Richard: Yes, I am listening. I want to make sure I got it right.

Jane: He says to back up slower.

Richard: I understand.

Jane: He is smiling about that one.

Richard: I understand.

Jane: Do not put so much stuff in your truck. You get it too over-loaded.

Richard: I understand. Yeah, you are right.

Jane: It is very dangerous. What, Dad? He says it slows down your stopping time.

Richard: I understand. He is right. He is always right.

Jane: He says he thinks it is cute that you drive with your arm out the window as he did.

Richard: Yes, I remember him doing that. His arm was always brown on that side. When did he drive with the dirt knob? Was that in Hawaii?

Jane: I don't know. Do you want me to ask him?

Richard: Yes.

Jane: He says it was the year nineteen thirty-nine.

Richard: He had one in nineteen thirty-nine?

Jane: Yes.

Richard: Wow, he was young.

Jane: Your grandpa Moe gave it to him and he put it on his bicycle.

Richard: When did he put one in the car?

Jane: You want me to ask him when he put one on the car?

Richard: Yes.

Jane: He said he got to drive the car in nineteen forty-two and he took it off the bicycle and put it on the car.

Richard: How old was he in nineteen forty-two?

Jane: He was almost twenty.

Richard: That is what I was thinking. Was he in Hawaii then?

Jane: How old were you, Dad? He is telling me how he remembers. He was nineteen. He was sixteen when he gets to drive but he got his permanent license when he was twenty-one. He took it off his bicycle when he was eighteen but the Grandpa would not let him use it until he was older. He did not let him use it until he was twenty-one. Yes, because you have to keep both hands on the wheel.

Richard chuckles.

Jane: He says he was a rebellious 'little tyke.'

Richard: He was?

173

Jane: Well, that is what he says. Not in a bad way.

Richard: I know.

Jane: He was rebellious in a teenager way.

Richard: Yes.

Jane: The very first one that he had was a clear one, a white clear one. It was special.

Richard: He still has it?

Jane: Yes, his mommy gave it to him.

Richard: I understand.

Jane: Yes. She said, 'Don't tell your dad, but you are big enough now.'

Richard: I understand.

Jane: He was her favorite son, he says. (Chuckling)

Richard: Was he?

Jane: I don't know. Should I ask his mom? Will I get in trouble?

Richard: No, I don't think so.

Jane: She scares me a little bit.

Richard: Yeah, I know.

Jane: She's ornery.

Richard: You think so?

Jane: Yes.

Richard: (Chuckling) Yes, she is a little bit.

Jane: Dad says, please, do not ask her.

Richard: Okay, don't ask her.

VISION 20 I HAVE A SPECIAL MOM

In this vision, I refer to Richard's Mother, Marjorie Jane Powers Moe, as 'She' or 'Mom.' The Kathryn referred to in this vision is Richard's sister, Kathryn (Kathy) Lane Moe.

Jane: Do you remember the old refrigerator that she used to have? It is not like the refrigerators now. She had cold milk in there in the bottles, instead of the plastic as you have now.

Richard: I remember the bottles.

Jane: She still likes that milk the best.

Richard: Well, that's the best kind of milk.

Jane: Yes.

Richard: Is that the kind the 'milkman' brought?

Jane: Yes.

Richard: Okay. I remember that.

Jane: He would leave it at the door in the morning.

Richard: That's right. The man would bring the milk every morning.

Jane: You would leave the old bottles out there and now and then, he would bring the chocolate milk.

Richard: Wow!

Jane: Kathryn loved the chocolate milk.

Richard: Yes.

Jane: Kathryn loves chocolate.

Richard: We drank milk often. It was good for us.

Jane: She says we should drink more.

Richard: Yes, I should. I understand. I will, Mom. I had a very special, Mom. I still do.

VISION 21 KATHRYN LIVED IN LAGUNA

In this vision, I begin the story with Richard's Mother, Marjorie Jane Powers Moe, and I refer to her as 'she' or 'Mommy.' The Kathryn referred to in this vision is Richard's sister, Kathryn (Kathy) Lane Moe, and the 'Daddy' I refer to is Richard's Dad, Kilmer Oscar Moe Jr.

Jane: She says you were always helping her even when you used to trip over yourself. You were so little trying to help her.

Richard: Yes. I remember all those times, Mommy. I remember all the camping trips. What did you put in the bean and bacon soup to make it so special?

Jane: She says little pieces of ham and a little bit of chopped up onion, which she would boil first. Then she would add little peas chopped up tiny and a little piece of clove. She would put that in right before the onion and that would give it a special taste. In addition, she would add a little bit of cream to give the soup a great flavor.

Richard: Wow, it was delicious. Would you like to go camping with us now, Mom?

Jane: She wants you to go camping in Newport Beach. She is going to tell me to do that.

Richard: I understand. Did we go camping there, Mom?

Jane: No, but she has been there. It is very beautiful.

Richard: Yes, Kathryn lived there for a little while.

Jane: Laguna Beach.

Richard: It was Laguna Beach. Yes.

Jane: That's what Mom says.

Richard: Newport Beach, Mom?

Jane: No, Mom says, Kathryn lived in Laguna Beach.

Richard: Where do you want me to go camping? Newport Beach?

Jane: Yes. They do not have camping in Laguna Beach.

Richard: Newport.

Jane: She told me to go to Newport Beach and I arranged the trip for you. The Mommy whispered it in my ear. It was supposed to be a surprise and she forgot it was a surprise. You're supposed to act surprised."

Richard: I see. I will.

Jane: Daddy says, 'Mom, that's a surprise. Don't tell your son surprises.'

Richard: Okay. All right, I am not going to tell. Therefore, I will be surprised.

Barney 'The Barn' Powers Moe

CHAPTER 10 BELOVED DOG, BARNEY

Kilmer Oscar Moe Jr. is a wonderful father. As his father did before him, Kilmer Jr. tried to teach his kids by example. Kilmer Jr. shared with his children some of the same lessons that he had learned from his own dad. One of the lessons Kilmer Jr. wanted his kids to learn, was how to pay their own way in life. When it came time for Richard to go away to summer camp for example, if Richard really wanted to go, he would go to his dad and ask him.

179

If Kilmer Jr. believed the trip to camp would be good for Richard, Kilmer Jr. would say, "Yes, Son, you may go to camp. I will pay half and you can pay the other half."

Richard could earn his half of the money working in his dad's machine shop. There was always plenty of work. Richard had to decide if he wanted to work that many hours to pay his half. More often than not, Richard took on the work. This would make Richard's dad proud and he was happy to give his son the other half of the camp fees.

When Richard turned fourteen, his parents decided to move their machine shop to Pismo Beach. The whole family loved it there, having traveled to that area to enjoy many a family vacation. Pismo Beach would remain their favorite place. Richard worked very hard as they prepared for the move. Working side by side with his dad, Richard helped Kilmer Jr. move everything they owned from their home and their business.

One day after they completed their move to Pismo Beach, Richard's Dad surprised him by announcing, "Let's go get you a dog." Richard's mouth flew open and he began jumping up and down because he loved dogs.

As a 'little tyke', Richard had a dog book, which he used to look at with a flashlight after everyone else had gone to sleep. Richard would hide under the covers and 'Oh', and 'Aw', over all the different breeds. Richard's favorite breed was the majestic German Shepherd.

On a day that Richard will never forget, his dad got out a copy of the Pennysaver and they found some puppies in San Luis Obispo, about a twenty-minute drive from their new home. Richard raced his dad to their Old International pickup truck and off they drove to pick out a puppy.

Upon their arrival, the breeder and her new litter of purebred German Shepherd puppies tumbled out of a barn to greet them. Richard was overwhelmed. With a full heart, Richard cocked his head to decide which puppy should be his. All at once, his eyes melted at the sight of this little puppy tripping over his own paws. The poor puppy's paws seemed to be bigger than the puppy was. Richard reached for the little guy and picked him up for a closer look. Looking into the puppy's eyes as he held him close, Richard smiled when the puppy licked his hand and secured his future. Richard cuddled his puppy closer and felt the puppy's warm nose against his cheek. The puppy, now with access to Richards face, began to give it a good licking.

His dad had watched this whole exchange with a smile on his face and joy in his heart. Richard turned to look at his dad. He loves his little treasure already and announces with pride, "This one Dad. This is the one."

Of course, Kilmer Jr. could already see this puppy was to become part of their family. As his dad made the deal with the breeder, Richard began to get out his wallet to pay his half. He was surprise as his dad held up one hand to say, 'Stop.' Richard looked at his dad but remained silent as he waited for his dad to explain.

With tears in his eyes and a catch in his throat, Kilmer Oscar Moe Jr. looked at his son. Kilmer Jr.

murmured, "This is a gift I want to handle. This puppy is my gift to you."

On the way home during this joyful journey, the new puppy slept with his head on his new owner's lap. Thinking nothing of it at the time, Richard had watched his new puppy eat a rather large amount of puppy food just before they left. Pulling into the driveway at his new home, Barney delivers his tummy ache onto Richard's pants. Richard did not care. He was just so infatuated with his little puppy, the one with the huge paws.

It was not until after his dad died suddenly that Richard began to wonder if his dad's idea of buying the puppy might have been a premonition; a premonition that Richard would soon find himself without a best friend. Richard's beloved Dad has always filled those shoes.

After his dad's tragic and sudden death, Richard turned to Barney as he looked for an answer to the new emptiness in his life.

Barney becomes Richards's new best friend, taking over where his dad had left off. Barney went everywhere with Richard. I asked Richard why he would name such a beautiful creature that carried himself with such elegance the name, Barney. Richard shared with me that not only did Barney have those huge paws, as Barney ran, this rather large tongue of his would drag on the ground, and he would trip over that as well. The only name that fit him was, Barney.

I learned the story about Barney and the trip to buy him from Kilmer Jr. Richard's Dad remembers this story like it was yesterday and it brings him mixed feelings as he retells this day in his son's life. Kilmer Jr.

did not want to die and leave Richard behind with a puppy in his place. These memories bring Kilmer Jr. feelings of sorrow. However, Richard's Dad is able to find some peace in his heart from the knowledge that after his own death, Richard had someone else to turn to.

The happiness that Barney brought to Richard is the kind of joy that only another pet owner can truly understand. Barney is in Heaven. He understands that someday he will reunite with his owner. With this in mind, beloved dog, Barney, waits for his Richard.

VISION 22 WHAT A GOOD DOGGY

The following is a recorded vision about Richard's beloved German Shepherd, Barney, who I refer to as 'he,' 'him,' 'doggie,' or 'Barney.' Richard is referring to Barney as, 'The Barn'.

Jane: I understand. He is going to chew it for me.

Richard: Well, you should chew a little bit.

Jane: No!

Richard: You don't want to chew the grass?

Jane: No, it's nasty. He gets it all waded up in his mouth drooling and....

Richard: Yes.

Jane: No, I do not want to.

Richard: He's getting it ready for you.

Jane: Barney is chewing the grass. He is putting the grass on my paw.

Richard: I see.

Jane: He's making my foot feel better.

Richard: Everybody's helping you, Honey.

Jane: It feels good.

Richard: I see.

Jane: Maybe I should chew some of that.

Richard: Try it.

Jane: Not yours, Barney, no, not that part. He has his paw up there on my paw, like that. What a good doggie!

Richard: I see. He's so smart.

Jane: I think I am going to call him Lassie.

Richard chuckles.

Jane: You don't like that. Let me see if Barney likes that. He does not. He is shaking his head.

Richard: He is, 'the Barn'.

VISION 23 BARNEY'S MIDDLE NAME

The following is a recorded vision about Richard's beloved German Shepherd, Barney, who I refer to as 'he,' 'him,' 'doggie,' or 'Barney.' Richard is referring to Barney as 'The Barn,' or 'Barn.' The 'Robert' I am referring to is Richard's maternal Grandfather, Robert Irvin Powers. 'Lady' in this vision is Robert's dog and 'Mom' is Richard's Mother, Marjorie Jane Powers Moe.

Richard: So you are going to see, 'The Barn?'

Jane: I am touching him right now.

Richard: I see. You got to the end of the tunnel?

Jane: Yes.

Richard: I see, great. Good boy, Barn.

Jane: I can see Robert.

Richard: Is Robert there?

Jane: Yes. Do you have a doggie, too? He has a doggie, too. Robert, is that your doggie?

Richard: What kind of doggie is it?

Jane: I do not know. Shall I ask him?

Richard: Yes.

Jane: He has a Cocker Spaniel.

Richard: I see.

Jane: Yes.

Richard: What is his name?

Jane: It is a girl.

Richard: It is a girl. What is her name?

Jane: I do not know.

Richard: Can you ask them?

Jane: I understand. 'Lady' is the dog's name.

Richard: 'Lady' is the dog's name. I see.

Jane: Is she registered? That is not her registered name. Barney, you are not registered, no, but we could.

Richard: Yes, he is a purebred dog.

Jane: Do not cry. It does not mean anything. It's just a name.

Richard: He is a purebred German Shepherd.

Jane: He says he's crying because that's his wife's name. That is the name of Robert's dog, too. He wants to be a registered dog so he can have a bigger name. He has a long name, though. It's 'The Barn' Barney Moe. That is the biggest name I ever heard of, for a dog.

Richard: Yes.

Jane: See, Barn? Okay, he wants a middle name. Let's call him Lassie.

Richard chuckles.

Jane: Let's called him, 'The Barn' Barney Lassie Moe. You like that. I understand. He does not want a sissy name. Barney wants a big name. Let's give them your name, your middle name.

Richard: My middle name is Powers, the same as Robert's last name, Powers.

Jane: I see, how about that one, Barn?

Richard: I would feel honored if he would have that name.

Jane: You like that one?

Jane: Now it is, 'The Barn' Barney Powers Moe.

Richard: I understand.

Jane: Yes, he likes that.

Richard: I do, too. The Robert should like that, too. That's his last name.

Jane: Yes, and that's your mom's last name, too.

Richard: It was her last name before she got married.

Jane: I see. Yes.

Richard: Yes.

Jane: Marjorie Powers.

Richard: Yes.

Jane: She does not like me to call her Marj or Marjie. She hates that. She wants me to call her Mom but I called her, 'the Mom.'

Richard: Yes.

Jane: Because that means the Mom.

Richard: Yes.

Jane: She hears me. That way I have respect for my Mom and then that gives her very best name too, 'The Mom.'

Richard: Yes, 'The Mom.'

Jane: Yes.

Richard: I understand.

Jane: Yes, she likes that.

CHAPTER 11 RICHARDS BEST FRIEND

Richard, "The next great gift that I've received from all of this is to learn that my dog, Barney, my German Shepherd that I had when I was fifteen years old, is in Heaven with Mom and Dad. I will tell you the story of Barney. When I was about fifteen I wanted a dog and my Dad said, 'Let's go get you a dog.'"

"We looked in the Pennysaver and we found an article for a German Shepherd, which was my favorite dog. It was about twenty miles away up in San Luis Obispo. Dad said, 'Let's go to San Luis Obispo.'"

"We went to see this litter of puppies. They were all so beautiful. I saw this dark, dark German Shepherd puppy and I pointed to that one, 'That's the one, Dad. That's the one.' I picked up that puppy and I loved him right away."

"Dad had always taught me to pay my own way. He usually paid for half and I paid for half. Most of my time growing up if I wanted to go to camp I'd say, 'Dad, I want to go to camp.'"

"Dad would say, 'Well, I'll pay for half and you can pay for the other half.' Dad had a machine shop; he always had work for me to do and he was trying to teach me lessons. That was what he did."

"When it came time to pull out my wallet, while I am holding onto this puppy, Dad says, 'Nope, Son, this is my present to you. I want to buy him for you.'"

"I don't know if Dad had a premonition, or if it was just bad luck, but Dad died less than a year later. Barney became my new best friend. Barney went everywhere with me. I worked on a dairy after my Dad died. I wanted to keep working during high school, so I fed three hundred cows every morning and every night."

"Barney would go everywhere with me. No matter where I went, Barney went. He was just my very best pal. I ended up moving to Los Angeles after High School and I could not take Barney with me because I was going to live at a friend's house. I knew it was only temporary until I got on my feet, but I had to leave Barney for a while with my mom. Barney stayed in Pismo Beach until I was able to get a house with my friend, Pete. Finally, it was time to bring Barney back."

"I drove up to Arroyo Grande to pick up Barney. I drove up in Pete's van, which Barney had never seen before. When I was about a half-mile away that dog's ears perked up and he started running down the road as fast as he could towards that van. Barney somehow knew that I was in there. It is just amazing how Barney could have known that. He was always that way. Barney always knew what I was thinking and he was always there to be protective of me. Barney is just one of those exceptional dogs. We always have one pet in our lives that is just so incredibly special. Barney was mine."

192

PART III BECOME AN ANGEL

CHAPTER 12 YOUR SPIRIT LEAVES

I have always said, "We are a Spirit and we have a body," instead of the usual reference made to how we are a body and have a Spirit. We do not have a Spirit; we are a Spirit who has a body. We use this body for its purpose here on Earth. We leave it behind when our body's die, but our Spirit continues.

I have learned from my Angels that they are more alive than we are. When we become an Angel, we keep everything we were before, including our personality. We are the same as we were within a body, but without the limitations, our bodies gave us.

When I visit Richard's family in Heaven, I feel no stress, only tranquility. Everyone in Heaven is the age each person wants to be. I have yet to see anyone in glasses, with no hair, or grey hair. There are no diseases, no mental problems, and everything is quite white or black. There are no gray areas.

For the women who desire make up they can have all they want and every brand they want. There is no need to reapply or touch up your make up, unless you want to. Once make up is applied, it always looks perfect, even while swimming or going under the waterfalls.

The men never had to shave; if they want a beard or a mustache, so be it. You can sleep if you want to but it is not required. You do not require food to sustain your body. You eat just for the pure pleasure it brings you. You can eat everything you want to and boy, do they! Scales do not exist because no one gains weight.

Heaven is all about God and the family. My Angels spend their time with their loved ones. They play, have fun, and tease each other and most of all; they love each other. Richard's loved ones have shared hundreds of stories with me.

These darling Angels love to tell, and retell, their favorite memories. As I am listening to their stories, I see a three-dimension reenactment of the actual event as it occurred. With amazement, I watch Richard as a 'little tyke' running around at a bowling alley, or Richard's Mom and Dad holding hands on their first date. As I watch these memories unfold, it makes it easy for me to re-share their stories with Richard.

The memories of life from Earth go with you. For example, the cove in Hawaii where Kilmer Jr. and his family grew up is an exact likeness of where they make their home in Heaven. From his memories on Earth, Richard's Dad has added his sailboats, his favorite waterfalls, the boars he used to hunt, and the very rock on which I land when I come to visit. Kilmer Jr.'s favorite items are still with him.

In Heaven, Richard's Dad has all the fish he caught during his lifetime: the fish from his childhood as well as all those from when he became an adult. Now Kilmer Jr. can fish no matter where he is; all he has to do is pull out his rod and reel and water will magically appear. Waiting in this water for Kilmer Jr. to catch them again are the Rock Cod, which Kilmer Jr. and Richard caught off the cattle boats. Also waiting are the Perch they caught in Mazatlan, Mexico, in the surf. Even the Sailfish and the Swordfish which Kilmer Jr. caught when he was a child in the Hawaiian Islands, magically wait for Kilmer Jr. to hook them again.

These fish are swimming around in the water that appears until Kilmer Jr. drops his line. With glee, these fish watch and wait until Kilmer Jr. begins to fidget. The fish know that this fidgeting is their clue to hop on his line. His fish love this game as much as Kilmer Jr. does. Can you imagine? How great it must be to go fishing and know that every time you drop your line you are going to catch a fish. These fish are forever with Kilmer Jr. and they are happy to bring him the same excitement and joy he experienced when he caught them the first time.

God so loves the world that all living things here on Earth journey with us to Heaven. Even the non-living can join you if it brought you happiness here. Kilmer Jr. still has everything he whittled in his cove, as well as his beloved surfboards. Every day the sun is shining and the weather is always perfect, not too cold, and not too hot.

While dominating the perfect wave, Kilmer Jr. surfs. Behind him, surfing on their own miniature surfboards, are Kilmer Jr.'s puppies, all his kittens, Marjorie's Parakeets, B.C., the Poodle, Cocoa, the Poodle, and of course, Barney. Giggling with delight, these animals race towards the shore as they all try to out-surf each other. This is truly Heaven.

Kilmer Oscar Moe Jr.

VISION 24 DAD'S FISH HAVE THE GIFT

In the following vision, I am referring to Richard's Dad, Kilmer Oscar Moe Jr., and I call him, 'Daddy,' 'he,' or 'Dad.'

Jane: Can you grab the rope?

Richard: I got it.

Jane: Do not tell Dad about the secret 'cause he's fishing.

Richard: No, I will not tell him.

199

Jane: It is a secret.

Richard: Okay, it is a secret.

Jane: Daddy catches the big fishes from down in Mexico.

Richard: Is that right?

Jane: Yes.

Richard: It's the same fish.

Jane: I think it is.

Richard: Wow!

Jane: He catches their brothers and sisters, too.

Richard: Really?

Jane: He gets to catch a whole bunch of them.

Richard: Wow.

Jane: He doesn't have to wait long, though. He just has to start fidgeting and once he fidgets then they know it's time to come and jump on his line.

Richard: I like that.

Jane: Yes, they know when he fidgets.

Richard: How do they know?

Jane: They have the gift.

VISION 25 YOU SET HER FREE

In the following vision, I am talking about Richard's Mother, Marjorie Jane Powers Moe, whom I refer to as 'she,' 'Mommy,' or 'Mom.' I am also talking about Richard's Dad, Kilmer Oscar Moe Jr., whom I refer to as 'Dad' or 'Daddy.' 'Kathryn' is Richard's sister, Kathryn (Kathy) Lane Moe.

Richard: Can you ask Mom something?

Jane: Do you want me to ask her that?

Richard: Can you ask Mom, when did she go up to the gift? Was it one year after she died?

Jane: She said you set her free.

Richard: I did?

Jane: Yes.

Richard: I did?

Jane: Yes. What does that mean, Mom? She said that she waited until she knew her loved ones were okay. You set her free.

Richard: How sweet is that?

Jane: She's saying, 'Ashes to ashes, dust to dust, when the time was right, I went to be with Dad.'

Richard: I see.

Jane: That's beautiful, Mom.

Richard: Yes, that is so beautiful. Did she go when we were up in the Bristle Cone Pines?

Jane: What did you say?

Richard: The Bristle Cone Pines.

Jane: The Bristle Cone Pines? Not until after Kathryn was ready, too. That was a long walk and she walked it with you.

Jane: (Weeping) I see. It is so painful. I feel all her pain...in my heart. It was hard for her to go.

Jane continues weeping.

Richard: We appreciate her staying until we were ready.

Jane is weeping still and the tape shuts off.

Kilmer Oscar Moe Jr.

VISION 26 WHEN DAD DIED

In the following vision, I am talking about Richard's Dad, Kilmer Oscar Moe Jr., whom I refer to as 'Dad' or 'The Daddy.'

Jane: The Daddy wants to tell you a story about when you die. When he died, it was an accident.

Richard: Okay.

Jane: Yes

Richard: I would like to hear that story.

Jane: What did you say, Dad? He says that you think you are sleeping. You don't know that you are never going to wake up again. When you die you go to sleep, then you go through the same tunnel as I go through.

Richard: Okay.

Jane: They see a large, bright light. Then they go towards that light. Dad sees everybody he loves that has already died. He sees his daddy, he sees his pets, he sees his grandpas, and he sees his grandmas. They are all waiting for him and he thinks to himself, 'Self, why am I seeing all these people in my dreams?' He does not realize yet that he died.

Richard: I understand.

Jane: They all hug him and kiss him. They all love him, they point down to him, and he sees himself. He is laying down there. He does not understand. How he could be up here when he is laying down there? Then all of a sudden, he starts to cry, because he knows. They take him into the light.

Richard: I understand.

Jane: Then he does not feel so sad anymore. He feels all the love that he told me about in the first dream, when he comes to see me. There is so much love. The baby Jesus is the big Jesus and he loves you so much.

Richard: I see.

Jane: Yes. He wants me to tell you that it is the best love that you could ever know.

Richard: That is beautiful, Dad! Thank you so much. Thank you for that story. Dad, after that you have to make your choices?

Jane: First, you have the reunion with your families for a while.

Richard: I see.

Jane: It is a very lovely time.

WHAT HEAVEN IS LIKE

Richard: I understand.

Jane: You do not have to make your decisions immediately. You wait for a while.

Richard: Good.

Jane: Yes. Then around our nighttime, you go and you see your life on the wall from Saint Peter. He talks to you about your life and they ask you if you want to have the gift now. Do you want to stay with your families and make sure your family is okay?

Richard: How wonderful is that.

Jane: That is when you make the decision.

Richard: I understand. That's a great story.

Jane: They are so happy to know that they can still come back and see their loved ones. They say, 'Can I talk to them?' St Peter answers, 'That is another long story.' St. Peter smiles very gently, because he always smiles like that, and rubs his beard. He doesn't have to have a beard. No one has to have a beard.

Richard: That's beautiful, Dad. Thank you.

Charlotte

VISION 27 CHARLOTTE & HER CHOICES

In this vision, I am talking to Richard about his sister-in-law's Mother, Charlotte, who has recently passed away. Richard's Sister-in-law is Cheryl Moe, who is married to Richard's brother, Robert Kilmer Moe. Richard and I refer to Charlotte as 'she.' When we refer to 'they' and 'you guys' we are speaking of Richard's dearly departed family. I begin the vision with Richard asking his mom, Marjorie Jane Powers Moe, about Charlotte.

Richard: Mom, Cheryl's Mom went to Heaven today. Is she up there with you guys?

Jane: Of course.

Richard: She's with you guys.

Jane: She's coming in. What does that mean? She is there; she has to make her choices.

Richard: Okay.

Jane: What does that mean? Sometimes, okay, sometimes it takes a while to be there and there are decisions to make, because there are so many choices.

Richard: I understand.

Jane: She's making those choices now.

Richard: I see.

Jane: She doesn't want to let go, yet. She is still making her choices but they feel her.

Richard: They feel her there?

Jane: Yes.

Richard: Okay.

Jane: They see her. She is not looking for them. She is still here.

Richard: I see.

Jane: Sometimes, sometimes it's hard to go.

Richard: Yes.

Jane: There are many choices and it takes a while to make them.

Richard: I understand.

Jane: After you make sure your family is okay, then you let go, and you have the Gift. That is very beautiful, Mom.

Richard: That's beautiful, Mom. It's wonderful to understand. That's very beautiful.

Jane: It's like seeing your shadow. You know you are there.

Richard: You have to make the decision.

Jane: You can't see your shadow unless you stand in the Sun.

Richard: I see.

Jane: If you don't choose to stand in the Sun, you cannot see your shadow. What does that mean, huh? Mom! She says that sometimes, Honey. She says things just like that.

Richard: You have to stand in the Sun?

Jane: No, she tells you the answer to your question in a riddle.

Richard: I see.

Jane: I can too understand! I see, okay, she says I'm too young.

Richard: You are. You're just a baby.

Jane: I understand. She's not sad. She's safe.

Richard: She's safe.

Jane: Yes.

Richard: Yes. Good. Good.

Jane: Does he remember that?

Richard: Does he remember what?

Jane: I don't know. Do you want me to ask him? She, yeah, she wants to know, do you remember how hard it was for her to let go?

Richard: Yes.

Jane: She says she had to make her choices, too.

Richard: She stayed here for a long time didn't she?

Jane: Do you want me to ask her that?

Richard: Yes.

Jane: She stayed until you were ready.

Richard: I thought so. Thank you, Mom

Jane: She waited until you were ready.

Richard: I understand.

Jane: She couldn't see your dad until she made the decision. I don't understand. You can see him right now. I see, I see, I see. She knew. She knew your dad was okay.

Richard: Okay, go ahead.

Jane: He didn't need her as much as you did.

Richard: Thank you. I needed her a lot.

Jane: She needed to know you were okay.

Richard: I know.

Jane: Okay, Dad, I will tell him. Dad says he stayed a long time, too, for a very long time.

Richard: I see. Thank you, Dad. Thank you so much.

Jane is still weeping.

Richard: It's okay, Honey. That is beautiful. That is beautiful. Thank you, Dad.

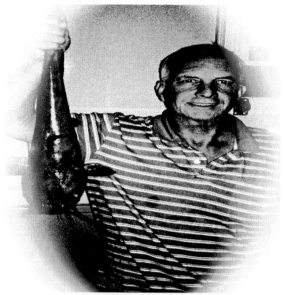

Richard Moe & His Catfish

CHAPTER 13 RICHARD POWERS MOE

My journey with the Angels has taught not only me about life after death, it has taught Richard as well. I have learned to communicate with the dearly departed in my dreams, and Richard has been able to use my sleep talking as a way of communicating with his beloved family. However, through our experiences with Richard's Angels, Richard has learned that he, too, can communicate with his loved ones.

Richard's parents have explained to him that they have never left him and that they never will. They can see him and hear him. More important, Richard has learned to hear his mom and dad as they guide him through life with love and nurturing.

Richard takes his dad with him to work every day. Richard talks to his dad; secure in the knowledge his beloved daddy can hear him. Sometimes his mom goes to work with Richard and his dad and sometimes she stays with me. Richard has learned to 'listen' to what his loved ones want him to know and it gives him such peace.

A recent example I can share: Richard was looking for a set of blueprints he needed for an important inspection at one of his construction projects. We had recently returned a rental car, my car was transporting Richard and me back and forth to the Solvang area so I could write this book, and Richard's truck was at another one of his projects. We were also using our motor home at the lake so I could have solitude in which to write. Richard does not remember in which of these vehicles his plans are in and for a brief second started to panic. Richard was sure they were in the motor home but we could not find them. I saw the look on his face and then a moment later it was gone. Richard, listening to his dad, understood that his plans were in his truck. No worries; he would see that they were there the next day when he went back to work.

Richard's family immediately eliminated the stress over something so important. Richard had the answer in his heart and did not let it worry him. Richard knew. This was such a positive change for Richard. Before Richard learned to listen to his loved ones he would have been in a panic; racing around worried and stressed all night.

Upon asking Richard what this experience has meant to him he replies, "I feel that I have more of a sense of purpose. That all the things we go through is for a reason. I know what Heaven is about now. It is about our loved ones and the memories we create on Earth. I have learned that we have to try to have as little regret as we can because that regret lasts for eternity."

Richard's Dad was his best friend. Before his dad's death, when Richard was only fifteen, they did everything together. Even Richard's career was secure before his dad passed on because the plan was for Richard and his brother, Robert Kilmer Moe, to take over their dad's machine shop. That opportunity was lost and Richard wandered for many years through different jobs, searching for an answer on how to earn his living. In losing his beloved dad, Richard lost his best friend, his career, and the man he so dearly loved. Richard also adds the following; "I want to let everybody know that they don't have to miss their parents; especially like I have missed my parents for so many years. I have them in my life again. How I wish I could have known this forty-two years ago. I am not so scared anymore."

Richard continues, "My mom and dad are here with me everyday. I can talk to them and I have learned that if you really listen, you can hear them. To have my family back in my life has given me a sense of serenity. I do not feel so lonely anymore. I know that I am not alone even when I feel stressed over something. I am not 'in this' alone."

"I would also like to tell people to take the time to smell the roses. Do not make the same mistakes I have, wasting so many years just hustling without taking time out for life along the way. I haven't got it all figured out but I am learning how to listen to those 'little voices' inside me that are trying to guide me in the right direction."

"I believe I am a better listener. In a relationship, I have learned to hear what my partner is saying. I know that just because you think you are right does not mean the other person doesn't have feelings or needs that you should listen to. It is important to communicate."

"I have learned to pray every day. I ask Jesus for guidance and help and I thank Him every day for my blessings. My parents want the message told that everyone should pray, every day. Mom and Dad have shared with me that when you say the name, Jesus, He is there. Jesus is everywhere."

"I also thank my mom and dad for being there for me. I thank them for Jane's visions for through her I have learned to develop by own gift of communication."

"I want everyone else to have their loved ones back and to cherish every second that comes their way. I know that my gift is different from Jane's, but it is still mine. I can talk to my family again."

"Every dream that Jane has is factual. Having no previous knowledge of these facts, Jane has told me so many details of my childhood, my parent's childhood, and my grandparent's childhood. Jane retells events that could have only come from my loved ones in Heaven. There is even a story that she recites about a motorcycle ride I took in my twenties, when drunk, in detail and I was the only one there. After Jane recalls this terrible evening, I learned that my beloved dad and Jesus were both with me that night. I always wondered how I made it through that night. Now I know I would not have lived through that experience without their help."

Richard communicates with the Angels on his shoulders differently than the way I do, but this is normal. Richard has learned to open his heart and his mind so that he can 'hear' what his loved ones are saying to him. Before my visions began, Richard had no idea his dad has always been there for him. Richard lost forty years with his dad because he did not know that his beloved dad had never let go. One magical day, however, Richard reached a turning point with his Angels. Richard began to listen to his loved ones while we are camping in the hills at Lake Cachuma, California.

Sticking his head in the door Richard asks me, "I am going to go fishing. Would you like to go?"

Looking at Richard I answer, "Which spot are you going to?"

With a shrug Richard responds, "The same one down at the cove."

It was a beautiful Sunday day but I was not feeling well so I tell him, "You go, Honey. I think I will just rest."

Richard sits down on the bed and changes his mind, "Well, I think I should stay here in case you need me. You just got over Bronchitis."

Looking at him, I give Richard some news I think he should have, "Go fishing, Richard. Go down to Harvey's Cove. Do not go to your usual spot. Walk down the stairs, turn to your right, and fish right there."

With a look of amazement, Richard cocks his head and asks me, "Do you have a feeling?" He is referring to my listening to his dad give me a hint as to where Richard should fish. I nod my head and without saying a word, Richard smiles, kisses me goodbye, and heads out our motor home door. With a wave, Richard picks up his rod and reel, his tackle box, and disappears towards Harvey's Cove.

I had no doubt that Richard would bring back a fish or two. What I was not prepared for was the look of total joy on his face as well as his announcement, "Come outdoors and see what I caught!"

Following Richard out the door to the patio, I watch as he proudly picks up the biggest Catfish I have ever seen and said, "You were so right. That is a great fishing spot."

With a smile, I take Richard's picture and off he goes to skin and clean his prize. Watching Richard as he heads towards the docks, I reflect on how much help his mom and dad have been, in so many ways. Later that night I remind Richard that he, too, can listen to his dad just as I do; he just needs to develop his own skills. Richard grows quiet with his thoughts but I can see the wheels turning.

Since that special Sunday, Richard has announced several ideas or thoughts that he now knows are not his, these ideas have come from his parents. Richard understands and treasures these new changes in his life.

I thank our wonderful, giving God every day for my visions. These amazing dreams are the answers to so many questions I had. My experiences with Richard's loved ones are a gift that I am able to give to the man I love. It is an incredible feeling to have brought so much joy and peace to Richard. He has his beloved mom and dad, his grandparents, his uncles, his aunts, his cousin, other family members, and his cherished dog, Barney, back in his life every day.

Knowing they will all be together again has given Richard a new purpose in life; one he is excited about sharing with everyone he meets. Richard is all about the Angels on his shoulders and he wants to make sure everyone knows about their own Angels in Heaven. Richard has promised his beloved families that he will help spread the word and share the lessons he has learned about his gift, a gift that he knows we all have. Richard does not want a single Angel in Heaven to miss their loved ones; the family they had to leave behind.

**Richard Powers Moe
At His Dad's Gravesite**

VISION 28 DAD WILL SWIM WITH YOU

In this vision, I begin the story with the word 'She' and I am referring to Richard's Mother, Marjorie Jane Powers Moe. I also am talking about Kilmer Oscar Moe Jr., Richard's Dad, and I refer to Kilmer Jr. as 'he' or 'Dad.'

Jane: She is going to make me well now.

Richard: Good. Thank you, Mom.

Long silence as Mom makes me well.

Richard: Is Dad there?

Jane: Yes.

Richard: Good. Can you ask Dad if he remembers when we went to the Saltine Sea?

Jane: He says he remembers as if it was yesterday. The waves were so big they crashed right around you.

Richard: Yes, I was scared.

Jane: He just picked you up and you thought it was so much fun.

Richard: chuckling. Yes, that was quite a trip.

Jane: He says you became a good swimmer.

Richard: Really?

Jane: He thinks so.

Richard: I see, well, thank you.

Jane: He says he built the swimming pool because he was so lonely for the water. He wanted the water close to him like when he was a little boy. That's one of the reasons he wanted the swimming pool built at the house.

Richard: Yes.

Jane: He missed the water.

Richard: He was the best swimmer.

Jane: He says he learned to swim when he was a little boy.

Richard: I see.

Jane: They went swimming to get food and to get things off the bottom of the Ocean. They would swim with the turtles, that they would swim with the fish, and that's how to swim. He learned how to swim because he learned how with his dad. His daddy was a good swimmer, too.

Richard: I see.

Jane: Yes.

Richard: Now he gets to swim with them again.

Jane: Yes, because they have the gift.

Richard: Yes.

Jane: He says he will swim with you again.

Richard: Wow.

Jane: He says he will swim with you again, someday.

Richard: Yes. I can't wait. I can't wait. I enjoyed all the times we went fishing, hunting, and camping.

VISION 29 DON'T DRINK & DRIVE

In the following vision I am repeating to Richard a question from his dad, Kilmer Oscar Moe Jr., whom I refer to as 'Dad,' 'he,' or 'Daddy.'

Jane: Do you still have the motorcycle?

Richard: No, I do not have the motorcycle anymore.

Jane: No? That is great!

Richard: Yes.

Jane: It's dangerous.

Richard: I know.

Jane: You drove too fast!

Richard: Yes.

Jane: You shouldn't drink and drive.

Richard: Yes.

Jane: You shouldn't drink and drive, especially on a motorcycle. That's what Dad says.

Richard: I know.

Jane: Don't do that! No, no, no.

Richard: No, I don't do it anymore.

Jane: Good

Richard: No, I don't.

Jane: That time you went around the corner; you went so fast you almost went over the side there. The Daddy was saving you. His hand, he's showing me, his hand was right there.

Richard: Was he?

Jane: He was right there around the curve. His hand was holding you.

Richard: Wow.

Jane: Do you remember that you were sliding?

Richard: Yes.

Jane: That's Daddy holding you.

Richard: Wow.

Jane: Yes, he was scared.

Richard: I needed him that night.

Jane: He was right there.

Richard: Yes, I know. I needed him. I was driving too fast and I drank too much.

Jane: Yes, that's what he says.

Richard: Yes.

Jane: Yes.

Richard: No, I quit riding motorcycles. Thank you, Dad.

Jane: He doesn't see one but he doesn't know if you still have it?

Richard: I sold it a long time ago.

Jane: I understand. He's so glad about that.

Richard: Good.

Jane: Yes, I am glad, too.

VISION 30 FUN IN HEAVEN

In the following vision, I am describing to Richard one of the fun things we are doing in Heaven. I am referring to Richard's Mother, Marjorie Jane Powers Moe, as 'she,' 'the Mommy,' or 'Mom.' Barney is Richard's beloved dog, which passed away when Richard was twenty-five years old.

Jane: Did you see that? They are going to fly in formations, the double turtles.

Richard: Do I see the turtles?

Jane: Do you see the double turtles? Yes, they have two layers.

Richard: I see. Do they hold each other's tails?

Jane: Yes! Yes, they fly in the formations. They are the baby turtles grown up now.

Richard: Did the baby turtles grow? Did they grow up?

Jane: They have babies themselves now to go with the one hundred and one kittens babies.

Richard: Are those the baby kittens the puppies are carrying?

Jane: Yes.

Richard: Yes?

Jane: The Barney is teaching his puppies to be very, very gentle.

Richard: Wow.

Jane: Yes.

Richard: Are you going to fly, too?

Jane: Yes. I am going to hold onto a tail.

Richard: You are.

Jane: Just like the Mommy does.

Richard: Mom does that?

Jane: Yes.

Richard: She probably holds up onto the fastest one.

Jane: She always wins.

Richard: I know.

Jane: It's her game, she says, so she can win.

Richard: I understand.

Jane: I know. I say, 'Let me win, Mom, let me win!' I just say that, like that.

Richard: I see. What does she say?

Jane: That you'll have your turn, dear.

Richard: Just like that?

Jane: Yes. She's going to make me sleep.

Richard: Is she going to help you sleep?

Jane: Yes.

Richard: Okay, good night everyone.

VISION 31 DAD READS UPSIDE DOWN

In the following vision I am talking about Richard's Dad, Kilmer Oscar Moe Jr., whom I refer to as 'Dad,' 'he,' or 'him.' Also in this vision, I refer to Richard's Mother, Marjorie Jane Powers Moe, and I refer to her as 'she,' 'Mommy,' or 'Mom.' The reference to 'they' is a reference to both parents.

Jane: The *'Old Lady Who Lived in the Shoe,'* that's one of your favorite books. That's what your dad read to you.

Richard: Yes.

Jane: Then you would count all the children.

Richard: How many were there?

Jane: Twelve.

Richard: Twelve?

Jane: Yes, because she had so many children.

Richard: I understand.

Jane: So she grew peanut butter and celery stocks. I don't think it goes like that, Dad. Geez, he's laughing about it.

Richard: Is he kidding with you or is he serious?

Jane: He's kidding with me.

227

Richard: I see. He's kidding with you.

Jane: They don't really grow the celery with the peanut butter already in it because you have to grow the peanuts.

Richard: Yes.

Jane: No, they don't. No, they don't. The peanuts do not grow inside the celery, do they, Mom?

Richard: Dad! He's teasing with you.

Jane: Yes.

Richard: He loves you.

Jane: He says they wrap around each other.

Richard chuckles.

Jane: I don't think so, Dad.

Richard: You're too smart.

Jane: That is so silly. Do you believe the story, Honey?

Richard: No, I do not believe that story.

Jane: He does not.

Richard: No, I do not.

Jane: He's laughing. He thinks he's so funny.

Richard: He is funny.

Jane: He's funny but he doesn't mean to be funny.

Richard: I see.

Jane: He's funny but he doesn't know it.

Richard: He is funny.

Jane: This time he meant to be funny.

Richard: I understand.

Jane: He's in a funny mood tonight. He'll tell jokes all night now.

Richard: I see.

Jane: Yes, and he'll pinch your mom.

Richard: I see.

Jane: Yes. He likes to pinch her when he's in a funny mood. He likes to pinch her. I can't tell you where.

Richard: I understand.

Jane: He pinches her cheeks, too.

Richard: I see.

Jane: Yes, he goes cheek, cheek, cheek, like that.

Richard: I see.

Jane: He puts his hands on both sides of her cheeks.

Richard: I see.

Jane: He does not pinch the cheeks down below. Okay, okay, Mom.

Richard chuckles.

Jane: He pinches the cheeks up above.

Both Richard and Jane are chuckling.

Jane: She doesn't want me to tell you those things because you're her son.

Richard: Yes.

Jane: She can tell me.

Richard: Well, I learned about my conception at the drive-in theater.

Jane: Yes, you did. No, I didn't Mom. No, it's our secret. No, I didn't tell him. I promise. Yes, just what kind of perfume you had on that night.

Richard: Yes.

Jane: That's all and the red lipstick.

Richard: Yes.

Jane: No, you told him about the no underwear. I didn't tell him about that part.

Richard: Yes, Mom, you told me that part.

Jane: Yes.

Richard: Yes, but I think it's cute.

Jane: She likes that story.

Richard: Yes, I do, too.

Jane: They were at the drive-in.

Richard: I know. I was a twinkle in Dad's eye.

Jane: Dad says they were the last one to leave the drive-in that night. (Laughing)

Richard: Can Dad read me a story?

Jane: I don't know. Do you want me to ask him?

Richard: Yes.

Jane: Okay, let me see what he says about that. He's looking through the books that he used to read to you.

Richard: Great.

Jane: So when she got older she broke in the glue, then... I can't say that part. I understand. The oldest boy's name was little boy blue, he stuck in his thumb, and it came out with glue? No, Dad, that's not the right one. That's two different stories. You're not supposed to tell the joke when you're reading the stories.

Richard chuckles.

Jane: No, cause I know better. I know it doesn't go like that. Mom, make him read the story right.

Richard chuckles.

Jane: No, and you're holding it upside down. No, Dad. He's so funny.

Richard: He is funny.

Jane: He won't...He wants to read the story upside down now.

Richard: I see.

Jane: I am not going to do that.

Richard chuckles.

Jane: I see, no, I'm not. He's saying it backwards now. I see, no. I can't say it like that...Blue Boy does. No, I'm not going to do that. You'll just wear me out.

Richard chuckles

Jane: He likes that book right there.

Richard: The Hat? I like that one. Read that story.

Jane: No, Dad, don't read it backwards. Turn it around. Turn it around like that. Put this side in this hand that side in that hand, hold it right there, and read it.

Richard: Dad, thank you for reading the book to me.

Jane: Not like that either.

Richard: Is he teasing with you?

Jane: Yes.

Richard: He loves you very much.

Jane: Do you want to hear about the Green Eggs and Ham?

Richard: Yes!

Jane: That's not a real book. There's no green eggs and ham.

Richard: Yes, there is.

Jane: He is showing me the book. The cat has his little fingers in there. He's holding a fork and he only has three or four fingers. That cat only has four fingers. Do you see? He's holding up a fork with the green eggs.

Richard: Yes.

Jane: The cat has a fork with the green eggs.

Richard: Yes, I want to hear that one.

Jane: If you read it right, I will. No, say it right, Dad. Start on that page right there, the first page.

Please? He says, 'Do you know it's a lesson for you, Son?'

    Richard: I know. I remember. It teaches you....

VISION 32 THE FLYING ELEPHANT

In the following vision, I refer to a 'she' and I am talking about Richard's Mother, Marjorie Jane Powers Moe. I also talk about 'Daddy' or 'Dad' and I am referring to Richard's Dad, Kilmer Oscar Moe Jr. Your 'brother' Richard's Mom is referring to is Richard's brother, Robert Kilmer Moe. Richard had planned a surfing trip with Robert, in Panama. However, Richard had to stay home and take care of me because I had a broken ankle.

    Jane: It's orange.

    Richard: Yes. What is it?

    Jane: The Peacocks are orange.

    Richard: I see. You have the Peacocks again.

    Jane: Yes.

    Richard: Are they at your zoo?

    Jane: They are in Zooloo land.

    Richard: I see. They are in Zooloo land?

    Jane: Yes.

Richard: Wow. Where did they come from? Did they come from the zoo?

Jane: Are you asking me did they come from the zoo?

Richard: Yes.

Jane: That's right.

Richard: Wow. What are their names?

Jane: I didn't meet them, yet. They are over there in Zooloo land. That is where we are going.

Richard: Is Zooloo land a part of the Zoo?

Jane: No, the Zoo is up by Mars.

Richard: I see.

Jane: You could see them from here because you have the binoculars over there.

Richard: Yes.

Jane: They hold on to each other's tails. They fly with their big ears. I am going to fly my Dumbo.

Richard: You are going to fly Dumbo?

Jane: Yes. He is all grown up now.

Richard: I hope so. Who's going?

Jane: Everybody is going to go up there for a good time.

Richard: I see.

Jane: Where are you?

Richard: I am with you right now.

Jane: No, he is with us.

Richard: Did Mom go for a walk with me today?

Jane: I do not know. Do you want to ask her? She said, of course. She loves to walk.

Richard: That was beautiful. Tell her I loved it so much.

Jane: She can hear you.

Richard: I see, yes.

Jane: She says she felt you so much.

Richard chuckles.

Jane: She was right there.

Richard: I could feel her.

Jane: She came back and forth. She came to touch me and then went back to touch you. Dad is fishing. He says he loves to go fishing on the big rock.

Richard: I know. I do, too. I am going to get a fishing pole this week.

Jane: Am I getting one, he says?

Richard: Do you want one?

Jane: I do not know. Where would we fish? Would we fish on the big rock from the 'whoosh?'

Richard: Yes.

Jane: I understand. Daddy says to catch the big eyes, the walleye.

Richard: I want to fish on the rock. The walleye fish are out on the boat, silly. He likes to catch the fishes from there.

Jane: What did you say, Dad? The big fish out in the ocean, they have little eyes while they are swimming around down on the bottom but when you bring them up to the top their eyes get so big. Daddy feels a little bit bad but not so bad, that he does not go catch them. (Laughing) Then we eat them, too. Mom fixes them and then we eat them.

Richard: You do.

Jane: Yes. Do you still catch those fish, Dad? Yes, he says he still does. Yummy, he loves them.

The Mommy says, 'Well, you did not go to see your brother.' She was waiting for you to go. She saw that you were going to go on the airplane. She was waiting and waiting for you to pack your suitcase but you did not pack it.

Richard: I know. I have too much responsibility. Too many people I need to take care of.

Jane: Mom says for you not to forget to take care of yourself.

Richard: I know. Thanks, Mom.

Jane: Mom says it is good to go for a walk and ride around the waters.

Richard: Yes, it makes my heart feel good.

Jane: She says it makes her heart feel good, too.

Richard: She still likes to go walking.

Jane: I know that, Mom. You walk fast.

Richard: Yes. Yes, she does.

Jane: She says for me not to walk yet because I could hurt my ankle.

Richard: Yes!

Jane: I could hurt my ankle. I am walking right now.

Richard: Yes, but you have to be careful.

Jane: I understand. She's going to ride the big elephant.

Richard: What is Mom going to ride?

Jane: She is going to ride the big, white elephant.

Richard: I see.

Jane: Yes, because she always rides the fastest elephant.

Richard: I see.

WHAT HEAVEN IS LIKE

VISION 33 WHITE SHOULDERS

In the following vision, I am telling Richard the kind of perfume his Mother, Marjorie Jane Powers Moe, whom I refer to as 'Mom,' wears. I also share with Richard what kind of cologne his Dad, Kilmer Oscar Moe Jr., whom I refer to as 'Dad,' wears.

Jane: They are going to have the kittens on their backs and say, 'Ride'em, cowboys,' like that.

Richard: Yes, the puppies will have the kittens on their backs and say, 'Faster, faster!'

Jane: Yes.

Richard: Do you know any of the names of the puppies?

Jane: The puppies do not have a name, yet. They have to earn a name.

Richard: I see

Jane: Yes.

Richard: That's interesting.

Jane: Yes.

Richard: Can the puppies get older? Do they stay the same?

Jane: What do mean?

Richard: Do they grow to get bigger? Do they stay the same size? Do they stay puppies all the time?

Jane: These puppies will get bigger because they got bigger when they were here on Earth with the lady on the farm. The only time a puppy remains a puppy in Heaven is when it died the size of a puppy here. The animals in Heaven get to choose their ages. However, their only choices are the ages between birth and the age at which they died.

Richard: I see, so they'll get big.

Jane: Yes.

Richard: I see, I see. I understand. They will get to be as old as they were here or they could be younger, too.

Jane: Yes. They can be whatever they want.

Richard: Yes. Are Mom and Dad back?

Jane: You can tell when they're coming because you can smell Mom's perfume.

Richard: I understand.

Jane: The *'White Shoulders.'*

Richard: Yes, Mom always wore the perfume called, *'White Shoulders.'* I used to buy it for her.

Jane: Yes, Mom wears that perfume and Dad wears, *'Old Spice.'*

Richard: Is that what he uses?

Jane: Yes, because I can smell it.

CHAPTER 14 THE PRESENCE OF ANGELS

You can communicate with your own Angels. As you can see from this book I communicate with the dearly departed in one way, Richard communicates in another way, and as you learn to use your gift, you will communicate in your own way. Everyone has this gift of communication with his or her loved ones. Your Angels understand this gift, they are eagerly waiting for you to accept it, and they are excited about sharing their new lives with you.

One night I asked my Angels about the other families I see in my visions. Can everyone talk to his or her dearly departed? Richard's family excitedly explained that everyone in Heaven wants to talk to those they love. They wait patiently for the chance to talk to those they had to leave behind. My Angels beg me to share my story, to spread the word of God, and help every loved one reunite with their Angels.

I talk in my sleep and Richard has used this ability to speak through me to his family in Heaven. What I can do with my gift in my sleep, for example, some of God's children can do while they are awake. We are all unique spirits, with our own unique skills, and Richard has learned to use his gift in his own way. You will learn to use your gift as well, in the best way that works for yourself and for your loved ones.

To learn to use your gift, I would like to suggest that you find a quiet place away from the everyday stresses of life. Go to a location where you can relax; if you have special place you shared with someone you lost, go there. Spend a night or a weekend at a cottage on a lake or treat yourself to a night at a hotel. Go for a walk along a quiet trail, sit in front of a calming fireplace, or curl up with a hot chocolate in your bed. The time it takes to feel your Angels does not have to be any longer than the amount of time it will take for you to relax.

Begin to feel God in the way that only you can. Sit very quietly and wait. Picture your loved ones and remember them in your hearts. Call out the names of those you want to talk to and tell your loved ones you are there. Let them know that you are aware they are with you, that they can hear you, and see you.

Listen and you will be amazed at what they tell you. Close your eyes and let them take you to a place where they can tell you so many things you want to hear. You will be surprised at how much they have to tell you, but most of all they want you to know that they are okay, they are happy, and they have never let go. They want you to know that they will be waiting for you when it is your time to join your loved ones in Heaven.

The depth of your experience with these loving Angels will depend on your openness and willingness to give them your energy. Each time you do this; each time you spend time talking and listening to your Angels, your gift will become stronger and more fulfilling. Although you may not be able to hear the voice you have come to associate with your loved one, you will notice thoughts that are new to you. A new clarity will emerge in your life. You will be aware of new answers and solutions as you go about your daily routine. You will always be able to hear your Angels, even on a busy street corner. The more you believe in your Angels, the more they can be there. They arrive on your shoulders when you call out their names so take the time to get to know them again. Talk to your beloveds all the time and they will be there all the time.

If you cannot hear your Angels the first time, relax. You will. The Angels on your shoulders need a chance for you to learn their art of communication. Talk to your loved ones all the time; when you say their name, they come to you. Take them to work with you. Explain any problem you may be experiencing with your loved ones. Often you will feel an answer from them in your heart. This answer will take you to a place of peacefulness and you will know they have found a solution for you.

Can you remember a time when you just knew you should have done something a certain way? Yet, you did not and after the event found yourself slapping your forehead and saying to yourself, 'I knew I should have done it the other way?' Can you remember a time when you thought to yourself or someone else, 'I just have a feeling such and such is going to happen' or 'I have a feeling I should be doing such and such?' You just experienced your Angels whispering in your ear trying to help you out. You heard them; you just did not know this 'little voice' inside your head is the voice of a loved one. You see. It is easier than you thought. You can hear them.

I am sure at some point in your life you have accomplished something special. Something, which you know, would have made your Angels proud of you. Do you remember how you felt at that moment? You felt his or her presence. Although they were not there in person, your Angels were watching over your shoulders, and sharing in your pride. Your loved ones were with you and you were indeed, feeling them. Now you can understand that your special Angels can be with you not just for a special occasion, they will be there as often as you wish. Your loved ones are reaching out for you; touch them in return by accepting them into your lives. Call out the names of your Angels every day, all day. Your loved ones miss you; miss talking to you and miss being with you, as much as you miss them.

Keep your Angels on your shoulders. Never let go of your loved ones. They have never let go of you and they never will. Remember; your loved ones are still a part of your life. Hold the hands of your dearly departed, just as you did when their Spirits were in their bodies. You can still feel their hand in yours; close your eyes and feel their words in your ears. Your Angels love you so much. Always remember; in whatever manner you develop your gift, you will find yourself in the presence of Angels, your Angels.

MEET THE AUTHOR

Jane Lea Dykstra

& FAMILY

Chanelle Dykstra Innis

Faith Dykstra

ABOUT THE AUTHOR

Jane Dykstra was born July 17, 1953, in Oskaloosa, Iowa. She attended college in Kirksville, Missouri, and studied English and Creative Writing. Jane was a member of the Alpha Sigma Alpha Sorority and Class Secretary for her sophomore year at Northeast Missouri State University.

Jane now makes her home in Newport Beach, California. She has one Daughter, Chanelle Fawn Dykstra Innis, and one beloved cat, Faith Dykstra.

Jane is the Daughter of Melvin E. Dykstra and Jeneane L. Dykstra. Jane has two brothers, Terry M. Dykstra, who is married to Peggy Swick Dykstra, and her younger brother is Daniel R. Dykstra, who is married to Grace Dykstra. Daniel's children are Kristina Dykstra, Desiree Dykstra, Jack Huang, and Dana Dykstra. Jane has one sister, Becky Dykstra, and Becky has two children, Michael Wanders and Tiffany Wanders.

Jane Dykstra is currently engaged to Richard Powers Moe and they plan to get married in 2012 in Oskaloosa, Iowa.